I0162006

Lorikeets

Lorikeets as Pets

Lorikeets Book for Keeping, Pros and Cons, Care, Housing, Diet and Health.
by

Roger Rodendale

Table of Contents

Introduction

Native to Australia, Lorikeets are counted among the most popular birds bred and kept in captivity. These beautifully colored birds are known for their large personalities and unique behavior. They are extremely entertaining birds which makes them very popular among bird enthusiasts as well as breeders across the globe.

For a long time, people shunned these birds as suitable pets as they had a very different diet and required special care in order to keep them healthy. However, with more information available about these birds today, they are not only kept in zoos and sanctuaries but have also found a very special place with people who love to keep birds as pets.

Although it may seem that these birds are yet another parrot species from the outside, they are quite different from the rest of the birds that are classified as parrots. They have extremely different dietary requirements and are even physiologically different from the others.

This book tells you in detail about the unique care requirements of Lorikeets. It is the ideal manual for just about anyone, be it a beginner or someone who has a good amount of experience with keeping birds as pets.

It takes you step by step through all the possible questions that you may have as a bird parent. The book covers important subjects like the anatomy of these birds, their natural habitat and range, the various sources that you can purchase your bird from, the housing and feeding needs of the birds, the different health issues that these birds tend to face and a lot more.

When you are planning to bring home a Lorikeet, preparation is the key to keeping them in your home successfully. You need to ensure that you have all the information that you will need to keep your bird healthy and happy. You must also be able to prepare your family for the possible challenges that come with keeping a bird at home as a pet.

What you can be assured of when you bring home a Lorikeet as a pet is that you will never experience one dull moment with this bird. They are extremely goofy birds who will entertain you all day with their antics.

These birds are also extremely intelligent, which means that they are easy to tame and train. You can socialize your Lorikeet quite easily and ensure that everyone who interacts with them will enjoy the company of these birds.

Lorikeets are known to be very friendly with humans. In fact, in several zoos, there are special Lorikeet exhibits where people walk among Lorikeets that fly freely in their enclosures. These birds also tend to get jealous when their humans pay attention to any other pets or even other people.

When you learn how to take care of your Lorikeet the right way, you will be able to enjoy several hours of petting and cuddling as these birds just love being handled. This book will show you the right way to take care of your Lorikeet so that you have nothing but great memories with your little companion.

Chapter 1) Introduction to Lorikeets

The exquisite beauty of Lorikeets is responsible for an increased interest in these birds among pet owners and bird enthusiasts. These birds are among the most colorful species and are small to medium sized, making them perfect pets as well.

Knowing the natural history and the physical appearance of these birds is the first step towards understanding the care that they need in order to thrive and be healthy. This chapter tells you all that you need to know about Lorikeets to help you identify these birds.

1. Physical appearance

Lorikeets are known for their beautiful plumage that makes them stand out from the rest of the parrot species across the globe. The colors of these birds can range from red, yellow, blue, violet, green to olive brown.

These medium sized birds have a long and slender tail that makes up for most of the length of their body. The head is round and has a flat crown like most parrot species. These birds are classified as true parrots because they have a characteristic hooked beak. The upper mandible curves over the lower mandible just like any other parrot species.

These birds are also called "brush tongued parrots" because of the unique shape of their tongue. As the name suggests, the tongue is shaped like a brush allowing these birds to eat pollen and nectar. The tips of the tongue have several fine hairs called papillae that almost work like mops to collect the nectar and the pollen from the flowers. They crush flowers with their strong beaks first and then use the brush like tongue to get to the food.

The brush like tongue allows the bird to collect all the pollen and turn them into small bundles that can be swallowed easily. These birds also have four toes that allows them to climb onto branches of trees. They can also perform several acrobatics thanks to their feet and the strong beaks.

Difference between a male and female
These birds are not sexually dimorphic. This means that you cannot tell the difference between a male and a female by looking at the bird. If you plan to breed the bird or if you are looking for a specific gender, then here are some simple ways to tell the difference between a male and female Lorikeet:

- **Observe mating behavior**
  When the mating season arrives, the males put on quite a show to lure the female. For instance, the male may hop around a potential partner. He will also stretch his body to its full length and will bob his neck up and down. While doing this, the male Lorikeet also emits low whistling sounds. This method only works when the bird is sexually mature, which is at about 18 months of age.

- **Keep an eye on the nesting box**
  It is needless to say that it is the female who will lay the eggs. But if you are not sure which one of the two birds laid the eggs, watch for the movement around the nest box. A female Lorikeet will spend all her time in the nest box. It is the male that will occasionally leave the nest box and come back in.

- **DNA testing**
  There are several labs where you can determine the gender of the bird with an egg shell sample, blood sample or feather sample. You will have to use freshly plucked feathers. You must also make sure that any pieces of the egg shell that you use is from ones that have recently hatched. If you wish to draw a blood sample, it is best that you take your bird to the vet. You can determine the gender of the bird at any age using DNA testing.

- **Take the bird to a vet**
  Of course, your vet will not be able to tell the gender of the bird through visual cues. A surgical process that is called endoscopic sexing is used to determine the gender of the bird. The Lorikeet is anesthetized to begin with. Then, an endoscope is lowered into the abdomen through the air sac. This is when the sex organs become

visible, allowing the vet to tell the gender of the bird. There are some complications such as infections that are possible with this process. In addition to that, this process is also a lot more expensive.

Difference between a lori and a Lorikeet
The difference between a lori and a Lorikeet is pretty much the same as the difference between a parrot and a parakeet.

The size is the first differentiator between the two types of birds. Lorikeets are smaller in size and have tails that are longer and more pointed. In comparison to this, the lories are usually larger in size with tails that are square or rounded and short.

Lorikeets are usually red in color with purple, yellow and green patches. Lories, on the other hand, are usually green in color and have small patches of yellow and red. Of course, with hybrids you will see many exceptions. In the wild, as well, these birds can come in a range of different colors.

2. Taxonomy
Lorikeets and lories have usually been classified under the subfamily Loriinae or have been classified as a separate family called Loriidae traditionally. It was in the year 1836 that naturalist and ornithologist, John Selby classified them as a tribe. However, none of these traditionally taxonomical classifications have been proven by any molecular studies.

According to most studies, it has been revealed that both Lorikeets and Lories have evolved from a single group that is related to fig parrots and budgerigars.

Under the Lorikeets and lories, two groups have been recognized. The first group includes the genera *Charmosyna*, which is more closely related to *Vini and Phigys* that are genera belonging to the Pacific Ocean. The second group consists of the genera *Eos, Chalcopsitta, Pseudeos, Trichoglossus, Psitteuteles, Lorius, Glossopsitta, Parvipsitta, Phighys, Vini and Neopsittacus*. One genera, called *Oreopsittacus*, is believed to belong to a third group altogether as per studies. The placement of this genera is still unknown.

3. Habitat and distribution
These birds are primarily arboreal. They are normally found on eucalyptus trees, mangroves and in forests. These birds fly from one place to another in search of food. They are also known to migrate from one island to

another. This is why there are thousands of Rainbow Lorikeets blanketing the sky across the coast of Australia during the flowering season.

Being arboreal also protects these birds from potential predators. Since they are small in size, they are easily able to hide in trees. The colors also act as camouflage in some cases, keeping these birds safe from predators like snakes and other birds of prey. These birds also tend to live in large groups to stay safe. They are constantly looking out for predators or any other danger and will warn their flock mates upon spotting any.

Depending upon the species, these birds hail from different parts of Australia and also parts of southeast Asia. They are found in large numbers in the Australasian range and can also be spotted in Polynesia, Timor Leste and Papua New Guinea. These nomadic birds are also found in several urban settlements in these areas and are considered a pest because they tend to invade vineyards and also coconut farms.

4. Natural behavior

These birds are known to roost in large numbers that can go up to thousands in number. They usually gather in these numbers at night. However, during the day, they tend to move in smaller groups or may even move in pairs.

As mentioned before, these birds are nomadic and will travel far in search of food. Almost 70% of the day of Lorikeets is spent looking for food and feeding. When they are travelling, the size of the flock is usually around 16 birds whereas, the feeding flock can be of about 20 birds. Although it may seem like a travelling flock consists of thousands of birds at times, it includes several smaller travelling flocks that are about to get back to the roosting area.

It is common for different species of Lorikeets to share the same roost. For instance, a rainbow Lorikeet is usually seen with scaly-breasted Lorikeets, little Lorikeets or Musk Lorikeets. However, these birds may compete with other birds such as starlings and mynahs for resting areas.

In seasons like winter and autumn, which is usually the breeding season, the non-breeding birds will be seen on a communal roost while the ones that are breeding will roost in the hollows of trees that consist of the nests.

These birds can fly up to 20 miles or 35km around the roosting area in search of food. In every range inhabited by these birds, you will see major and minor roosts. The major roosts are usually seen with a gap of 70km between each other. The minor roosts appear in between these major roosts. The minor roosts are temporary roosts and are the ones that they may share with other species.

These birds are active during the day and will return to the roosting areas prior to sunset. Even after these birds have returned to their roost, there is often a lot of commotion as the birds settle into their specific positions for the night. There are some members of the flocks that will roost during the day. These birds will preen the roosting area and will remove twigs and leaves that are unwanted from the branches.

Lorikeets roost in large numbers for several reasons:

- There is more security from potential danger when they are in large numbers.
- Single birds are able to find mates when they reach sexual maturity in these large flocks.
- They are able to share any information about different food sources. This helps them keep an eye out for new food sources as well.
- Newly hatched birds can remain in the care of parents while the other flock mates provide for them. This allows a breeding pair to teach fledglings the different feeding techniques, how to choose food and other things that inexperienced birds need to learn.

These birds can even chase out large birds from their nesting areas and feeding areas if needed. They even compete with birds that they usually roost with incase the food resources are scarce.

It is very easy to spot pair bonding between Lorikeets. These birds are known to mate for life. A bonded pair will spend a lot of time preening one another and will also nibble at each other. These birds are known to display some aggression towards other birds that are non-pair birds by protesting and even biting at times.

5. Aviculture of Lorikeets

Unfortunately, most parrot species that are bred in aviaries in the United States may be destined to be sold for pet trade. There are several species of birds that are not meant for aviculture. The Lorikeet, however, is one bird that is perfect for aviculture because:

- It is colorful
- It is active
- It has a great personality

This is also the reason why these birds not only make the best aviary subjects but great pets as well. Since a ban has been imposed on the import of these birds in most parts of the world, only captive breeding that is USFWS approved makes it possible to produce these colorful birds in these regions.

The type of Lori or Lorikeet that is bred depends upon how good the bird is as a pet. Some species can be extremely unfriendly and can exhibit behavior such as biting. Others make wonderful pets and can even get quite talkative and vocal. In fact there is a type of Lorikeet called the Chattering Lorikeet, which is known for its ability to talk. The latter are the birds that are usually chosen to be bred in aviaries.

Another feature that makes these birds wonderful aviary subjects is their hardiness. Most of them can even be kept in outdoor aviaries in winters when they are given the right type of shelter. In fact, there are several pictures that show these birds rolling around in the snow even though they originate in the warmer parts of the world. However, some birds, such as the ones that belong to the genus *Charmosyna,* may not be the best to keep in aviaries in colder parts of the world.

The biggest problem arises when the breeding season begins. Many species breed in the month of January, which can be quite harsh on the hatchlings in the cold conditions. Any dampness seen in the nesting area can be harmful for the chicks, which makes it necessary to change the bedding and substrate every single day.

Lorikeets are also great aviary subjects because they are not as messy as other species of parrots. They do not leave any seeds or food droppings on the perches and the floor. The droppings of most species of Lorikeets are completely liquid and can be absorbed easily into the substrate. You can simply change the substrate or hose of the floor of the cage every day.

There are some drawbacks of having Lorikeets in aviaries, of course. One of the biggest ones is that housing more than one pair in each cage can be quite a task. You may breed a single male with multiple females without any issues. However, having pairs can lead to fights for resources.

Lorikeets seldom do well with other species of birds in the same aviary. It is possible to have different varieties of Lorikeets together, however. Although they are small, these birds tend to be extremely dominating by nature. They are capable of bullying even the largest birds in the aviaries when they need to. So, you need to be especially careful if you wish to introduce smaller birds into the aviary.

Lorikeets are known to be extremely aggressive and may even enter fights that can be fatal for the other bird. This makes them a difficult bird to keep in aviaries unless you are able to learn about the different varieties of Lorikeets that are compatible with each other. These are the ones that are most likely to roost in the same spot in the wild.

Of course, the demand for Lorikeets as pets makes them a great option for most aviaries. However, if you do wish to breed these birds for commercial purposes, it is necessary to obtain a license. In the USA, you can obtain a license from the American Lory Society or the International Loriinae Society.

You can get regular journals from these organizations as well. That keeps you updated on the care requirements for these birds along with the different breeding methods that are applied today. It is, however, a good idea to look at an aviary as an option to interact with these wonderful birds instead of making it a mainly commercial venture.

6. The pros and cons of having Lorikeets as pets

Having a Lorikeet or any other feathered pet, comes with its share of pros and cons. Knowing about them in detail will help you decide if you will truly be able to commit to one of these birds which can live up to 20 years or more in captivity.

Pros of having a Lorikeet as a pet

These birds are complete clowns. They love to perform for their owners and family. You will not have a single dull moment with the acrobatics and antics of the bird. This, coupled with their tweets and, of course, the gorgeous plumage is something that you can enjoy all day long.

These birds are extremely curious and inquisitive by nature. They will explore different items around your home to pick things that will cause them no harm. Then, they will make a toy out of any of these items.

You can also purchase several toys for them to play with. For instance, foot toys, hanging toys or even just a cardboard box can make for wonderful toys for these birds.

If you are looking for a pet bird that loves to be with you and cuddle, these birds are the ones that you need. They are complete attention seekers and will love to accompany you during various chores around the house.

The good thing about these birds is that they are not as messy as other parrots. They consume nectar for the most part which means that you do not have to worry about seeds being flung around the enclosure.

These birds love to play rough. You can roll them on their back and even nudge them around to play with them. They will nibble at your fingers and even clothes gently to invite you to play. They love to play with their brush-like tongue and will sometimes stick it up your ears as a way of showing affection.

These birds do not shed as much feather dust either. So, if you have people at home with allergies, then these birds are ideal for you. They are not as destructive as other species of parrots.

Cons of having a Lorikeet as a pet

The highly specialized diet of these birds is one of the biggest concerns for most pet owners. These birds are nectar eaters for which they even have a specialized tongue as discussed before.

These birds do not have a beak that is as strong as other parrots which makes it hard for them to eat seeds. They also tend to fall extremely sick when they are given a diet with seeds. These birds also need a diet that is very high in carbs because of their high energy levels. They also have a very fast wing span that requires this type of food.

You can get several wet mixes commercially that are designed especially for Lorikeets. However, these foods spoil easily and are also extremely expensive. You will have to replace the food from the bowl frequently to prevent any chances of bacterial infections.

Just like other fruit and nectar eating birds, Lorikeets are always at the risk of Iron Storage Disease. You need to provide them with enough iron supplementation to avoid this.

The process of digestion with Lorikeets is quite different in comparison to other parrots. Because their diet predominantly consists of nectar, the poop is often very watery. The flip side to this is that it can splatter very often. They also tend to poop all over the place at times.

These birds are highly susceptible to yeast and bacterial infections because they have a diet that is high in moisture and also because of their short and weak GI tract. This means, you will have to prioritize hygiene and make sure you never miss cleaning the cage daily of all the poop and any other mess.

Besides this, Lorikeets can get extremely hormonal. This may include sudden nipping and biting. Although the beak is smaller and softer, they tend to latch on to your finger when they bite, making it quite painful.

You need to be prepared for a noisy family member when you bring home a Lorikeet. They will make loud, shrill and long roosting calls at dawn and at dusk.

Although they are extremely trainable birds, they can be stubborn too. So it takes some patience when it comes to training your Lorikeet. If he or she decides that they do not want to do something, it is almost impossible to bring them around. This stubbornness when coupled with aggression can become quite a task for owners. They tend to have extreme mood swings and can go from being cheery to nippy in just a matter of seconds.

These birds are extremely territorial. They are so territorial that they will risk getting into fatal fights as well. So, when you introduce new birds into your aviary, you need to be extremely cautious if you own a Lorikeet. It is best that you house them in pairs that have bonded with each other. It is also a good idea to have the same species of birds in one cage.

This territorial behavior aggravates when your Lorikeet is hormonal and can lead to some ugly fights. So it is best that you avoid bringing birds of other species into your home when you have Lorikeets.

To sum it up, the Lorikeet is not the ideal bird for you if you are a first time parrot owner. However, if you do want to bring one home, make sure that you learn as much as possible about these birds. There is a lot of hardwork involved when it comes to parenting a Lorikeet. You can expect a lot of love and affection from these birds nevertheless. But be prepared to have a member in your family who wants all your attention all the time. In the end, though, Lorikeets can be really rewarding pets for your entire family.

Chapter 2) 5 Things to Prepare Before Buying a Lorikeet

You can never be too prepared for your Lorikeet. These birds are extremely sensitive to change. So, when you bring them home, they can be quite stressed. To ease this transition, you need to be fully prepared to make sure that your bird is comfortable in your home.

1. Keep the housing area ready

You should have the enclosure of your bird ready before the bird is home. That way, he will have a secure space for himself to get used to his new surroundings.

The first thing you need to ensure is that your Lorikeet gets lots of space to fly around and really spread his wings. This is because these birds cannot manage any other form of exercise such as climbing on cages. So, when you are setting up your baby's permanent home, you need to be very aware of the space you are providing.

The size of your enclosure must be at least 30 inches in length for a pair of Lorikeets. You should worry about the length more than the height of the cage. The rule of thumb is that the length MUST be greater than the height.

The distance between the cage bars also matters. Since these birds are small in size, the spacing between the bars should be between ¼- ½ inches. If the cage is wider or narrower than this, you put your bird at the risk of injury.

Make sure that the cage is made from material that is non-toxic and durable. You should also be able to disinfect this material easily. The ideal option is aluminum. It is best if you can get a cage made from aluminum with a PVC powder coating. You also have the option of plastic coated cages. These cages are easy to clean and will also come in a range of colors.

The next thing to keep in mind is the design of the enclosure. No matter how fancy the cages may be, if they are not accessible, you will not be able to maintain them well. Every nook and cranny of the cage should be easy for you to clean. The cage door should be positioned in a manner that allows you to reach out for the bird when required. You must also make sure that you may be able to add more birds in the future to avoid the ordeal of transferring your birds to new cages.

It is always a good idea to keep Lorikeets in pairs, as they need the company of another bird in order to thrive. In case you decide to have more than two birds, you also need to remember that one of them will be dominant and may attack cage mates that are submissive. The best way to ensure that this is avoided is by accessorizing your cage well and making sure that the birds have ample visual barriers to keep themselves safe from any attack.

Number to size ratio
There are a few rules that you need to follow when choosing the size of the cage that you want to keep your bird in. There is a value called the bird number to size ratio. In the case of Lorikeets, you should be able to provide about 3-4 inches of floor space for every pair of birds that you want to house.

The height of the cage is not really important, as it does not really interfere in the personal space of each bird. What is important to note is that the movement of Lorikeets is mostly horizontal and rarely vertical.

Of course, if your cage is very tall, the birds will like to take the highest perch to rest themselves. This is the only vertical space that the birds will fight for. In general, Lorikeets will opt for the perches and the vertical space if they do not have ample floor space to move around in.

The ideal size for a cage for your Lorikeets is 6ft x 2ft x 3ft (length, depth and height). This should be able to accommodate three pairs of birds easily.

Here are some things you must NOT do when you are buying a cage for your Lorikeets:

- Do not go for enclosures that are too decorative and intricate in design.

- Make sure that the cage does not have many crevices that will be difficult for you to clean in the future.

- Cylindrical cages should be avoided, particularly ones that are small in their diameter.

- There should not be any gaps that may trap the feet of the birds.

- Watch out for paint that may peel off from the cage or from the perches or other items on the cage.

- Do not get any decorative items that use treated wood as they may harm the bird.

You have the option of building your own flight cage in case you do not want to invest in large cages that can be very expensive.

Building the enclosure on your own
There are various types of aviaries that you can build including outdoor aviaries or full wire aviaries. The designs and plans are easily available on the Internet. However, you need to have some basic considerations before you actually construct an enclosure for your bird.

You can get a wire enclosure constructed for as little as $10 and this is the most economical option available. This can be a super fun project. All you will have to do is dedicate a little time towards it.

The best type of aviaries to build are the free standing ones and not the permanent ones. That way it is also easy if you decide to move. Now, the only thing you need to remember with any permanent structure is that you may have to get permissions from Zoning departments in your area.

Here are a few things you must consider before you construct an enclosure for your birds:

- Make sure you find a good location that is free from any traffic and noise.

- You should have access to water and safe electrical outlets.

- If the enclosure is indoors, you need to make sure that you give the birds ample air flow in order to be healthy.

- Indoor enclosures should be built in a way that they are easy to clean.

- You need to make sure that an outdoor aviary has good drainage. This will ensure that there are no damp floors, which may lead to disease.

- In the case of the outdoor aviaries, it is also important to ensure that the area is safe from any pests or predators.

17

- As discussed before the enclosure should be longer and not taller. You need to be able to provide ample floor space to each bird. A simple measure of 4 sq.feet per pair should help you understand the size of the aviary.

- The cage door is the trickiest part of the enclosure. You need to make sure that it is easy to access while keeping the birds safe from any chance of escape.

After you have taken care of all these considerations, the next thing to do would be to make sure that you get the right material to construct the enclosure with. Here are a few tips to help you with that:

- You can get all the material that you require from any home development store.

- The material that you purchase should be safe and must be free from any toxins.

- It is best that you avoid the use of redwood, cedar and screen wood. Pressure treated wood should also be avoided.

- Any material that corrodes such as brass or copper should be avoided.

- Zinc and lead may lead to heavy metal poisoning. These elements are usually found in the paints used to construct the cage.

- If you must use galvanized hardware cloth, make sure that it is washed with vinegar fully.

- Furniture polish and metal polish must be avoided at all costs when you make the enclosure.

- It is a great idea to get PVC powder coated wiring because of the ease of maintenance.

- Plastic netting is only suitable for indoor cages, as the outdoor ones will have rodents chewing into them in no time.

- Wiring should not have spacing more than ½" and less than ¼".

- Never use screens, as the nails of the bird will get caught in it leading to serious injuries.

The only other rule that you must keep in mind is to make the cage as large as you can afford. That way, your birds will have a lovely permanent home that they can live for the rest of their lives in.

How to position the enclosure
The most important thing with the enclosure is where you position it. You need to keep the safety and comfort of the bird in mind at all times. One thing with birds is that they tend to get really nervous if you tower over them all the time. The best way to position these cages is such that the perches are above your own eye level.

If you have placed the enclosure indoors, it is a good idea to have the enclosure near a window that can give the birds natural light. You also need to have a shaded area in the enclosure that the birds can rest in.

You need to make sure that the settings of the cage mimic natural light as closely as possible. If you need to provide artificial lighting, it is best that you provide full spectrum light. You need to set these lights to a timer that switches it on at dawn and switches it off at dusk, basically matching the sun rise and sun set. You will have to make seasonal adjustments to match the length of the day.

Lighting is the most important thing for your Lorikeets as it plays an important role in the hormone cycle of the birds. This influences breeding.

You can opt for fixtures that emit UV light, as UV light plays an important role in Vitamin D production and also calcium absorption in birds. You have to make sure that the cage is dark at night. Opting for a dim light is also a good idea to prevent any episodes of night fright.

There is no need to cover your cage at night. It is has been discouraged by a lot of bird lovers and owners as it can reduce the amount of fresh air that your bird gets. Also this may upset your bird's sleeping cycle, as they may not wake up with the rising sun.

The area that you choose to house your birds in should not have temperature fluctuations. The kitchen is one such example. You should also make sure that the area is not accessible to your other pets and is also free from any toxic plants. You can get the birds acclimatized to any temperature that is comfortable for you. All you need to make sure is that it does not fluctuate too much.

If your birds are going to stay outdoors, shade is absolutely necessary. If you live in an area where the temperature fluctuates, the cage should be placed in an area that is protected from this fluctuation. The plants that are around your aviary should be non-toxic and bird friendly.

It is absolutely mandatory to keep free ranging birds away as they may contaminate the food of your birds and also spread infectious diseases.

With these tips and ideas, you should be able to find the ideal space for your aviary. That way your birds are not only safe but are guaranteed to be happy in the area that they are going to spend the rest of their lives in.

Accessorizing the cage
Stimulating the bird and making sure that he gets ample exercise is one of your biggest responsibilities. The perches and accessories of the cage are essential not only for the physical exercise but are also important for feeding the birds and giving them ample visual barriers if you have multiple birds in your aviary.

The type of perch that you choose plays a very important role. If you opt for dowel perches, you may face issues like lack of foot exercise as the bird may not get proper footing. These perches force the birds to shift all their weight on to one foot. As a result, in case there is an outbreak of bumblefoot, it may get aggravated.

Dowel perches may be included but should not be the only perch in your cage. Opt for perches that are made from nontoxic hardwood and clean material.

If you are planning to get a branch for your cage, make sure that it is obtained from a tree that has not been sprayed with any pesticides. Wood rot and mold should also be considered when you are bringing wood from the outdoors. The best option is to purchase manzanita branches that you will find in any pet store.

Although some people may tell you that sandpaper covered perches are good for your bird as it keeps the toenails short, you must never opt for this. It leads to foot infections and bruises.

You must also place the perches such that they are not directly above one another or directly above the food and water bowls. This prevents any chances of contamination due to the droppings. Make sure that perches made of wood are replaced regularly as they become contaminated with time.

The next most important cage accessories are the food and water dishes. The only thing you need to remember is that these dishes should be very easy to clean. The best option for Lorikeets is a stainless steel cup. Metal containers having soldered ends should be strictly avoided as they may lead to lead poisoning.

The water and food bowls should be placed away from one another to encourage exercise. If you notice that your bird is nesting in the cups instead of feeding from them, you will have to shift to a tube style feeder.

Lorikeets will also appreciate a place to roost in at night. A nest or a perch should do the trick. You can place it near the upper corners of the cage. If you make a roosting area with wood, avoid cedar and redwood or any other pressure treated wood. You can use shredded paper, coconut fibre or tissue paper. Remember that this roosting area will also encourage breeding among your birds.

The nesting or roosting area is not mandatory. However, if you have several birds in your aviary, getting sleeping tents for birds also gives them a good hiding area in case one or more of their cage mates become aggressive.

When it comes to accessories for Lorikeets, less is more. You have to make sure that the area is not too crowded. Flight should be comfortable as this the most preferred form of exercise as far as Lorikeets are concerned. This is also the most effective way of exercise for Lorikeets.

2. Bird proof your home

Many bird owners make the mistake of putting off the process of bird proofing their home until after they have trained the bird to get out of the cage. This is a big mistake. You can never rule out the possibility of a chance escape when you have the cage door open for feeding or cleaning. If your house is not bird proofed, then you may have fatal consequences. So, when you decide to bring home pet Lorikeets, the most important thing to do is to make sure that your home is safe for them. This process is almost like baby proofing a home.

The first thing that you need to do is get rid of your polytetrafluoroethylene pans or Teflon pans. You must at least ensure that the kitchen is far away from the enclosure if you want to continue to use them. You see, when these utensils overheat, a certain gas is emitted. This gas is toxic for most birds, especially parrot species. Some iron boxes and room heaters also use this material. Make sure that your bird is away from them.

Then, you need to remove any lead items from your home. They are commonly found in wall paint, the curtain weights, some imported artefacts or even the enclosure of the bird itself. Lead is poison for Lorikeets. So, when you are buying a cage, make sure that you test the quality out first. Also things like the curtain weights become common objects of interest for birds. So, get rid of them.

Smoking indoors is prohibited if you have Lorikeets. They are extremely sensitive to any pollutant in the air. In fact, in the earlier days, people took birds like canaries when they went mining. If there were any pollutants in the air, the birds would react to them immediately. Your Lorikeets may develop pulmonary diseases if you leave them exposed to secondary smoke. If the bird picks any nicotine tar on its body, especially the feet, it becomes so noxious that it actually chews on that part and injures itself.

Toilet seats should always be kept down. There are many instances when birds have drowned in toilets. With tiny birds like the Lorikeet, this is more likely to happen. So, be extremely cautious.

All the wires should be concealed. Usually, they are the favorite toys for your Lorikeets. Tugging and biting electric cords can have serious repercussions. If your birds can fly, they may even get cut or injured by flying straight into these wires.

If there are any plants in the space occupied by the Lorikeet, you need to confirm that it is not poisonous for your bird. You may call the National Animal Poison Control Center Hotline on 800-548-2423/900-680-000. These calls will cost you about $30 per call. They can tell you if a particular plant is poisonous or not. If you unable to confirm this, get the plants away from your bird's immediate environment and wait until you have spoken to an avian vet before you put them back.

In case you have not had your birds wings clipped, you need to take additional precautions. You need to remove large mirrors to prevent any flight related injury. Ceiling fans must be removed or kept off unless you know that the bird is in the cage. Windows should be covered by a curtain. Birds that fly into windows or mirrors can injure their necks very badly. Of course, windows should be kept closed at all times to prevent any escape. This is the biggest cause for pet loss.

Lastly, you must be very careful about the stove or any other hot surface like the radiator. You should be able to find covers for these surfaces to ensure that your birds do not get burnt or scalded.

If you have other pets like a cat or a dog, you must keep them in a carrier or keep them chained. Cat saliva is toxic for Lorikeets. Also, if your cat or dog is not properly introduced to the new family member, they will most likely attack them. As for the Lorikeets, they do not stand a chance of survival when attacked by these animals that are natural predators.

3. Learn about the food requirements of your bird

The biggest concern for most Lorikeet owners is nutrition. In the wild, these birds eat only pollen and nectar. However, in captivity they may be fed with fruits, flowers, berries and buds. They do not eat seeds. The cardinal rule is that your Lorikeet will require food that is very rich in its moisture content. They also have a very short GI tract which means that they will eat and poop around the clock. You can expect them to have droppings in just 15-20 minutes of having a meal.

What to feed Lorikeets?

You have several substitutes for pollen and nectar that you can give your Lorikeet. You can mix these commercially prepared substitutes and give it to your Lorikeet in small amounts twice every day. Some popular brands include Avico Lory Life, Quicky Lory, Nekton Lory and CeDe Lory food.

You can give your Lorikeet several fruits and vegetables as well. You can dice them and offer it to your bird. Fruits must be included as a major portion of the diet. It is better to use over-ripe fruits that are soft for your Lorikeet. Cut them into small pieces as per the size of your Lorikeet. When you offer fruits and vegetables, make sure you give them to your bird in separate bowls.

Sometimes, your pet may begin to prefer a certain type of fruit or vegetable. If this happens, cut it out of their diet in order to introduce variety. You can later add the fruit or vegetable when your bird begins to eat others too.

Vegetables should be given in restricted quantities. It is better to give your Lorikeet pale green fruits and vegetables such as lettuce or celery as they are high in water composition. Make sure that you avoid avocado, as it is toxic for birds.

Any fresh produce should be washed thoroughly to ensure that there are no toxic chemicals on it when you offer it to your bird.

Your bird will have to have access to clean drinking water all day long. Make sure the water dishes are cleaned thoroughly as the birds may also take a dip in it occasionally to clean himself.

Supplements for Lorikeets

It is best to talk to your vet about the supplementation needs of your bird. If you are giving your Lorikeet nectar food as a major portion of the diet, supplementation is not really required. You may have to provide specific supplements during the breeding season. For instance, calcium is needed when your bird prepares to lay eggs.

Besides that you do not have to include extensive supplementation in your Lorikeet's diet.

4. Make sure your family is ready

In order to make the transition of your bird stress-free, it is not enough for you to understand what your bird needs. Every member of your family should be prepared for the arrival of the bird. This avoids any chances of unpleasant incidents with the new bird. The way you handle the bird, interact with him and maintain the ambience for the first few days plays an important role in the bird's well-being.

Here are some instructions that you should give all your family members before you bring the bird home:

- There will be minimal interaction with the bird. Lorikeets are extremely beautiful birds. So it is natural for your family members to want to touch and handle the bird. This should be avoided until the bird settles. You must make sure that they do not even speak to the bird for the first few days.

- There will be no visitors till the bird is completely comfortable. Too many new faces and voices can lead to a lot of stress for the bird. If you are planning parties and get-togethers, make sure you put it off until your new bird begins to look calmer and more composed in his new environment.

- You will not play any loud music or keep the television on at high volumes near the bird. This can disturb the bird and lead to health issues related to extreme stress.

- If you have children in the house, make sure that you tell them not to tease the bird. The Lorikeet is generally a very calm bird. However, when startled or approached roughly, they may nip as a means of self-defense. Lorikeets are large enough to cause serious injuries to children.

- Make sure all your family members are aware of the basic care and requirements of the bird.

- Another family member besides the one who has brought the bird home should have access to an emergency number. This includes the number of the veterinarian, breeder or any other animal helpline that you may have to contact in case of an emergency.

Work together as the new bird's flock to make him feel more comfortable. The more you work towards improving the bird's experiences for the first few days, the more likely he is to form a bond that is entirely trusting.

5. Find an avian vet

You never know when you may have a medical emergency with your Lorikeet. These birds require specialized experts to provide them with correct medical attention. So, make sure that you have found an avian vet in your vicinity even before you decide to bring the bird home.

So, what is an Avian Vet?

Veterinarians often specialize in one species or type of pet. While most often they are taught to deal with common pets like horses, cows, dogs and cats in vet school, exotic pets are studied separately as an elective. An individual who has studied birds, including the exotic ones, is called an avian vet. They would also have to spend several years practicing in facilities that deal with these birds specifically.

Veterinarians who specialize in specific rare species are part of the Association of Avian Vets. Since the Lorikeet is not a rare breed, you don't have to specifically look for a vet who is part of the AAV. It is, however, an advantage if you find one who is.

Finding an Avian veterinarian

The first source would be your breeder or the pet store. You can try the recommended vet but do not just assume that he or she is the best for your pet. In fact, many breeders and pet stores may have tie ups with the veterinarian in order to void your health certificate.

The best sources to get information about avian vets in your locality would be:

- ✓ Online or local bird clubs
- ✓ A regular veterinarian's office
- ✓ Good and reputed pet stores.

However, the best source to find avian veterinarians is the Association of Avian Vets. You can log on to their website www.aav.org or call the Central Office in Florida on (407)393-8901. They also have an active page on most social networking sites that can help you even find fellow Lorikeet owners in your locality.

It is worth knowing that some avian pets may also treat other exotic creatures like reptiles and amphibians. This does not make them unreliable avian vets or less informed in comparison to those who deal only with birds. Of course, you can ask them how much of their practice is dedicated to birds to make sure that they have enough experience with handling them. In case they are handling just up to 2-3 birds in a month, you can ask them to recommend someone who deals with birds mostly.

You can even casually ask your vet about interesting avian seminars in your city. They should be informed about this if they are interested in learning and educating themselves about birds. A good avian vet will probably attend a few himself.

The next most important question is whether they are available 24X7. If not, what would they recommend in case of an emergency in their absence? Then you also have to do some research about the hospital they recommend. If the avian vet you are meeting does not have this back up, look for another one who does.

How to know that your Vet/ Hospital is inexperienced?

It is not enough that your vet is educated about birds, even his support staff should be fairly informed. There are some signs that will tell you if your Avian vet hospital is really experienced or not:

- When you call for an appointment, they will tell you that it is too cold to bring your Lorikeet out instead of telling you how you may keep him warm on the way.

- The staff does not know what type of bird you have. They should definitely be able to recognize a Lorikeet as it is such a common pet.

- The staff is afraid to handle the birds, especially baby birds.

- Your vet examines the bird through the cage. He should do a correct physical exam to check your bird properly.

- The vet does not measure your Lorikeet. This is the first thing they need to do.

- They will not discuss basics like the bird's diet with you. Most avian problems are related to malnutrition and the first thing a good veterinary hospital does is find out all details about that.

- The appointments are not longer than 15 minutes. A good examination will take at least 30 minutes. So, if they are simply scheduling appointments every 15 minutes, they are probably not doing a thorough job.

- They do not recommend annual check-ups. If the vet tells you that you need to bring the bird in only when there is a problem, you need to show concern.

Basics of a good facility

Take a tour of the hospital or clinic to see how well the place is equipped. Here are some basics that are definitely available at any serious Avian Vet facility:

- A gram scale to measure the weight of the birds accurately.

- A good diet for the birds who have been hospitalized including pellets, fruits and vegetables.

- Incubator cages

- Separate rooms for the birds if they are also dealing with other animals like reptiles or even cats and dogs.

Once you have found a good vet

A good veterinarian is your most important support system in dealing with your Lorikeet. Stick with them always and make sure that you follow their instructions with respect to your bird to the last letter. If you are not cooperative, the help they can provide is very limited. Of course, you can call them about concerns you have about your Lorikeet but don't make this a habit. If you want to discuss something, fix an appointment.

Chapter 3) Where to Get a Lorikeet?

The right source for a Lorikeet is extremely important. It will determine the health as well as the behavior of your bird. The more reliable the source, the better the condition of your bird will be.

Here are the most common sources for Lorikeets discussed in detail.

1. Breeders

There are several Lorikeet Breeders in all the areas where these birds are popular pets. You can find a breeder near your home by looking up websites like www.birdbreeders.com that carry listings of some of the most popular breeders in your locality. If you are not one who relies on Internet searches, you can even ask a bird store owner to help you find one. You can even speak to fellow Lorikeet owners to introduce you to the breeders that they work with.

The advantage of getting your birds from a breeder is that they are likely to be healthier. You see, most breeders will focus on one type or family of birds. They will spend a lot of time learning about them and putting together the best breeding practices to produce healthy babies. You have various scales at which people practice Lorikeet breeding. Some of them just have a backyard breeding business and others choose to do this on a more professional level. Either way, you should be able to find a healthy bird if you find a good breeder.

Now, you have several breeders who will sell these birds through online stores. That is acceptable only if you are certain about the reputation of the breeder. Otherwise, it is recommended that you pay at least one visit to the facility to check the breeding conditions. There is one golden rule of thumb when it comes to breeders: If the environment is clean, the birds will be healthy. Check how the cages have been maintained, see if there is clean water for the birds and also understand how much these breeders actually interact with their birds. That way you can be certain of not just a healthy bird but also one that is social to some extent. Here are some handy tips when you are choosing a breeder to buy your bird from:

- Check for their experience. It is mostly suggested that you opt for breeders who have been in the business for a good amount of time. They will have experience with respect to various issues faced by bird owners and will become a valuable source of support for new bird owners. Of course, there may be some new breeders who are extremely passionate about their birds. In such cases, check for how much experience they have with managing and handling Lorikeets, be it their own pets or pets of friends and family.

- Check if they have an avian veterinarian. This is very critical. Every good breeder will be associated with an avian veterinarian. That is how they are able to have the birds regularly examined to give you some guarantee on their health. If the breeder does not have an avian veterinarian that he or she can recommend, you may want to look for new options immediately.

- The breeder must follow the closed aviary concept. That way you can be sure that the birds that come to your home will be disease free.

- Check the breeder's website. If you have come to know of a breeder through an email or a flyer, you must check for a website immediately. All good breeders will have one and will tell you in detail about their breeding practices on these websites.

- Look for recommendations. This is undoubtedly the best way to find a reliable breeder. You can ask the breeder if you can talk to other Lorikeet owners that he or she deals with just to understand how they have been able to cope with the bird. In the process, you will know if the owner and the breeder share a good relationship or not. If the breeder is hesitant to connect you to their customers, it is a sign of something fishy.

A breeder who truly looks out for his birds will also be a valuable part of raising your Lorikeet. He or she will be able to help you with all the initial preparations that you need to make in order to welcome your pet Lorikeet home. Along with a vet, your breeder is the only support you will need to raise a healthy bird in your home.

What is a Closed Aviary Concept?

This is a common practice among most bird breeders to ensure that the birds are free from any diseases. They follow strict quarantining rules to prevent any germs from entering their flock and damaging the health of the birds. There are a few rules that are followed with the closed aviary:

1. Usually new birds are not added to the flock: In case there is a need to add a new bird for whatever reason, they make sure that it is quarantined for a minimum period of 3 months and a maximum of 6 months.

2. The birds that are taken to the vet are quarantined too: Now, the chances of catching infections and diseases are high at the vet. So, breeders quarantine them to ensure that they do not bring back any air borne viruses. Even at the vet, these birds are usually covered with large towels to reduce the risk of infections.

3. They keep all birds out of the premises: That means they do not allow their friends, customers or anyone to bring birds in. Even rescues are not permitted unless there is a chance to quarantine them first.

4. They do not go to any place where there are other birds: This includes pet stores and even bird shows. They definitely do not take their birds there. And, in an event when they themselves go to one such event, they will take a shower and change their clothes fully before handling their own aviary. They do this to ensure that there are no chances of any indirect contact resulting in infections.

Breeders with these practices can be trusted as they invest a lot of energy to keep the health of their birds at its peak.

2. Pet Stores
You will be able to find several specialty stores that deal in birds alone. These are the most preferred source for your Lorikeet. Most such pet stores have a lot of information about the birds that they are selling. This will make the process of bringing a new pet home much easier for new owners. You need to enquire about the history of the bird that you choose just to be clear that the pet store has enough information about what they are selling you. They should be able to tell you a little about the general behavior of the bird, its parent and even a little about the breeder who they deal with.

Examine the conditions that these birds are living in very carefully. If you see that the cages have not been cleaned well and the water contains feathers of bird droppings, it is an indication that the bird may be unhealthy. This also shows that they have not been given enough attention which is a sure sign of behavioral problems. Ask if the pet store will offer any sort of health certificate. Some of the good stores will be able to give you a minimum guarantee on their pets.

It is alright to bring a bird home from the regular pet stores as well. As long as they have been cared for, you have nothing to worry about. When dealing with pet stores, you may want to do a little research about them and even shop around a little before you finalize a bird for yourself.

In case you plan to have a Lorikeet shipped to you, whether from a breeder or an online pet store, ask for the following:

- Pictures of the specific bird that you are going to get. Close ups and several angles are a must.

- A valid return policy in case the bird does not meet the right health expectations.

- Testimonials from clients and also a possible chance of interacting with them.

3. How to identify healthy birds

The first sign of good health is the posture of the bird. A healthy Lorikeet will be erect in its posture. They will also be alert to the slightest sounds and actions. They have a very clear look in the eyes that makes them appear sharp and intelligent. The feathers are tight with no bald spots. When in an aviary, no other bird besides the mate is allowed to peck the bird.

How to examine a bird

Most breeders and pet store owners will let you examine the birds. Make sure you wear soft gloves because a bird that is not used to you will peck and bite. Take a good look at the bird all the way from the tip of the beak to the tail. Here are the signs of good health:

- The beak should be able to close fully. It must be smooth all over the surface.

- The head should not have any bald spots. Unless the bird is molting, bald spots indicate poor health and breeding conditions.
- The wings should not have any broken shafts in them.

- You must examine each leg of the bird, separately. The toes should be straight with all the nails. There should not be any broken nails. In males, especially, toenails are extremely important. If you want to buy a pair of Lorikeets that you may breed in the future, a male without toenails is a problem. His poor grip will not help him mate properly.

- The tail must be neat and clean.

- Feel the breastbone of the bird. It usually extends from the middle of the breast to the bottom. On the either side of this bone, the flesh must feel firm.

- The cloaca or the anus of the bird must be examined. If you find sticky substances or any dirt in this area, it is an indication of possible intestinal problems.

- Breathing should be even. If you hear any peculiar sound, like a squeak in the breathing, it indicates a respiratory problem in the bird.

- Lastly, blow on the feathers of the chest and the stomach gently. If you see that the skin is healthy, it means that the bird is healthy. On the other hand, if you notice any redness or blotching, it is the sign of skin problems or infections.

Now, if any bird has one or more of the above problems, it does not mean that he or she will die quickly. There are several health issues that can be cured with minimum care. So, if the breeder or the pet store has been recommended by a friend or family, don't just dismiss them when you see any of the signs mentioned above. Tell your breeder and have the bird examined by a vet. It may not be a good idea to invest in a bird knowing that it is trouble. However, if your breeder can guarantee recovery, it is a good idea to consider it. If the breeder has been recommended by several bird owners, he will be great support for you in the future.

Birds that come with health issues need a lot of care. They may also be poor breeders. So, if you want to breed your birds, make sure that you pick the best quality stock.

4. Health certificates for birds

Getting a health certificate for a pet bird is mandatory. This is a guarantee of sorts on the health and quality of the bird that you are bringing home. For Lorikeets, your health guarantee is valid for a 90 day period. In that time, if the health of your bird deteriorates, the breeder will give you a replacement or will return your money. Any breeder who practices good husbandry will give you a health certificate by default. If he or she hesitates, you may want to reconsider your options.

Note: If you are ordering a bird online, you may not be able to avail a health certificate. This is because the health problems may be caused due to the shipping conditions that the breeder has no control over.

Here are a few conditions that you will see in any bird health certificate:

- The bird should be checked for any health issues within 72 hours of the purchase. Usually, you need to consult a vet recommended by the aviary. However, if you can find a breeder who lets you choose the vet, it is a better idea, as you can be sure of no internal connections.

- If any illness is caused because of poor conditions that you keep the birds in, the health guarantee will not cover for it.

- Accidents are not covered by the health insurance. This includes any attack by your existing pets, fires, smoke etc.

- No veterinarian costs will be covered by a health insurance.

- Behavioral issues in the birds will not be covered in this insurance.

- In the case of Lorikeets, any incompatibility between the birds will be covered in this insurance in case you are buying them in pairs. This is especially true when you are investing in a bird that is expensive.

When you get your birds examined, if the vet is able to determine the presence of any health condition that may be bacterial, viral or genetic, the breeder must give you a replacement.

For first time bird owners, it is a good idea to consult a friend who already owns a bird with respect to the conditions mentioned in the agreement. Normally, there are aviculturists who will offer this service at a small price. If you have no experience with Lorikeets, this is a good option for you. They will not only be able to verify the terms and conditions but also the health of the bird that you are bringing home.

5. Adopting a Lorikeet

Not everyone is equipped to take care of a pet bird. For this reason, and many more, people give Lorikeets away to shelters almost every day. In some cases, these birds are rescued from homes that are abusive as well. You can approach a rescue shelter in order to adopt your pet Lorikeet.

Of course, adoption is recommended for someone with some experience with birds. However, if you are willing to put in some effort into raising your bird, you will be able to manage a rescued bird even if you are a complete beginner.

This is one of the noblest ways to find your companion for life. Adoption is quite simple as every organization has a set of rules and guidelines that you need to follow to bring home your pet bird. Here is a step-by-step guide to adopting a Lorikeet.

When it comes to adoption, there are two options, you can either approach a rescue or you can approach a shelter. While they may seem like the same thing, they are quite different in reality.

Procedure for shelter adoption
A shelter is a facility that is run by the local government or by a non-profit organization. These are public facilities such as the pound and the animal control. Of course there are some private facilities as well. These are usually referred to as humane societies or clubs. They usually have more branches.

These shelters are either government funded or are run by individuals or a group of people. Shelters work like an organization and have dedicated staff and even fixed hours for working. There are also several volunteers who assist with adoption and general operations at these facilities.

You can look for sources to adopt your bird from online. There are dedicated websites that will give you details about the closest shelters to your home. They will also give you details on the birds that are available at these shelters.

With most of these shelters, the number of volunteers and staff is very low. That is why calling them to make enquiries may not be the best idea. Instead, you should visit them during their working hours. The details of the working hours are generally provided on the official website of each of these shelters. The websites will also list the birds that are up for adoption. If you can spot a Lorikeet among the listings, the next thing to do is to visit the shelter.

The procedure for adoption varies from one shelter to the other. The overall process is quite similar however. Some rules that you need to be aware of before you adopt a pet bird:

- The first step is to find a bird that you would like to adopt. Go through the listings provided by the website of the shelter.

- Paying a visit to the shelter to see the bird is a must. There is usually a reception desk at each shelter where you can get all the details of the bird that you want. You can even interact with the bird for a while to understand the personality and the temperament of the bird in general.

- You may have to pay an adoption fee in some shelters. This fee ranges from $20-$100 or £5-£50. It is entirely dependent on the shelter that you plan to adopt from. Also, the more medical attention the bird may have needed after rescuing him, the higher the fees. This is primarily to ensure that any medical attention that is needed for the bird is covered.

- Once you have decided upon the bird that you want to take home, you will have to give them a valid ID. Shelters also have a mandatory house check. With exotic species like the Lorikeet, illegal trading and breeding is always a threat. These house checks are mandatory to ensure that the bird is going into a good home. The goal is to prevent any chance of trauma if the bird needs to be rescued again and has to go through the whole process all over.

- You will have to complete the necessary paperwork. This will include details of vaccination and will also provide other health records of the bird.

- Make sure you spend some time with the bird before you decide to bring him or her home.

Procedure to adopt from rescue facility
The term rescue is refereed to an individual bird who has been rescued by someone and is currently under their care. These birds can also be cared for in a private boarding facility. Some facilities are run by volunteers and have regular adoption events.

When looking for listings for adoption, a rescue listing can be contacted immediately. You can even send them a meeting. If it is a private boarding set up, you will have to fill out applications and complete their adoption procedure.

Some rules that apply to rescues include:

- You can send an email or connect with the rescue with the contact details provided. Rescues are quick to respond and will call you immediately.

- You will have to provide all the necessary details about yourself. You can get all the details about the bird that you want to rescue through this conversation.

- When you are sure that you can handle the responsibility of the bird, you can visit the shelter or one of their adoption events.

- A home check is necessary when you adopt from a rescue. Only when the rescue is convinced that your house is a suitable environment for the bird will you be able to adopt.

- Once you have chosen to adopt the bird, you will have to submit all the necessary ID proof. You will be handed over the health reports of the bird as well.

- In case of an adoption contract, it has to be signed and the adoption fee should be paid. This fee is between $100-$300 or £50-150.

What is the difference?

While the philosophy and the objective of rescues and shelters is to make sure that the birds get a good home, they differ quite greatly in the processes that they follow.

With a shelter, you have the option of looking at different birds before you make the final choice of which one you take home. Shelters have a more stringent process. However, some of them will let you take the bird home the day you approach them for adoption.

Adopting from a shelter is definitely a much cheaper option. However medical expenses are higher in the case of a shelter.

When you adopt from a rescue, you have better access to all the information about the bird. The bird is also more cared for as it gets individual attention. However, with the adoption process you will see a lot more involvement from a rescue.

Since you are able to gather all the information that you need about the bird, it also means that you will find one that is more suited to your requirements. In case of a rescue, the adoption fee is higher. However, you do not have to worry about veterinary costs with a rescue.

When you adopt a Lorikeet, be prepared for certain behavioral issues that stem from the fact that the bird may have had a history of abuse or several illnesses. For adoption, it is always recommended that you have some experience dealing with Lorikeets or some type of parrot.

6. Baby bird or adult?

This is a common problem that new bird owners face. They are unsure if it is a good idea to bring home a sexually mature bird or a baby. Well, they both have their pros and cons. It is up to the owners to decide what kind of care they are willing to provide for the birds. Then, it is easier to choose between a baby and an adult. Here are the pros and cons of each:

Baby bird

Housebreaking is much easier with baby birds. These birds do not come with any baggage or behavioral issues. So, they are most likely to adapt to a new place faster. Most baby parrots require hand feeding for the first few days. This is true for Lorikeets too. So, if you are bringing a baby home, you need to learn how to handle them and feed them as well. It is also demanding in terms of time, as babies need a lot more care.

With baby birds, you also have to understand that their bodies are extremely delicate. This means that you may injure the bird when you are handling it. In addition to that, any slack in care can lead to infections. You also have to deal with the problem of moulting at about 8 months of age. This is when the birds can be very irritable and nippy. It is almost like dealing with a human teen.

The biggest advantage of bringing a baby bird home is that you can teach them your ways easily. They come with an empty slate and will be able to pick up the exact behavior that you expect from them. You can regulate the eating habits, timings for food, socialization and several other factors.

Adult birds

You will call a bird an adult when it has become sexually mature. In the case of Lorikeets, this can happen anytime between 8 and 12 months of age. Usually, an adult bird is trained to do a lot of things. So, that is a big responsibility that is lifted off your shoulders. Now, this also means that you will have to worry about the behavior that these birds come with. If they have any signs of aggression or depression, it will take you a lot of time to get rid of these problems.

When you bring an adult bird home, you have to remove him from an environment that he or she is used to. This can be extremely stressful for the birds. You can expect an aggravation in behavior issues if any. You at least need to prepare yourself to make the extra effort to help the bird get used to you and your home.

The advantage with adult birds is that they are easier to handle because they are well developed and not as weak as the babies. Health wise, you only have to worry about preexisting conditions. With the right care, they are less prone to infections and diseases in comparison to the baby birds.

Chapter 4) Common Questions About Lorikeet Behavior

The more you learn about your bird's behavior, the better the bond forged between you and your pet. Lorikeets are extremely intelligent creatures like any other species of parrot. This can even make their behavior challenging at times for most people to understand. Here are some common questions about Lorikeet behavior that you may also have along the way with your bird.

1. What behavior to expect on the first day?

It will take your bird three days or less to get used to the new home and surroundings. In that time, do not force your love upon the bird. They will treat you like a threat if your stand over the cage and try to talk to them or look at them. Whenever you approach the cage, make sure that you are at the eye level of your bird. This will teach your bird that you are an equal who means no harm.

On the first day, you will not talk to the bird or even go near the cage except to feed him or change the lining of the cage. At this time, the bird will either go away from you or will try to bite and nip. So, wearing gloves is a great idea. Even if your Lorikeet nips or screams, be calm. Pretend like he does not exist and just get on with the cleaning or feeding. When you are done, calmly close the door and walk away.

Around day 3, you can introduce yourself to your bird. Just place your hands on the sides of the cage and sit before the bird at his eye level. Do not move or talk. Just wait till the bird approaches your hand. He will nibble and even lick your hand. The idea is to get the bird used to your smell and presence. With hand-bred birds, you can even do this on the second day.

When your bird is a little comfortable, try to stroke the head through the cage. If he backs off or struggles away, then stop immediately. If he is comfortable, however, you can introduce him to your voice. Say hello to your bird in a very gentle tone. Don't talk too much. Just a few words should be enough just to introduce the bird to your voice.

Try to bring home a few treats for your bird. Your breeder will be able to tell you what treat the bird responds to the best. Treats are a great tool to reduce stress. They will also make the bird approach you voluntarily.

For the next few days, keep the interaction with your bird limited. Just go about your daily business. Whenever you are approaching the cage, say hello to your bird. Lorikeets are a species of parrot. So, you must expect these birds to be highly intelligent. Even when you are not interacting with them, they have an eye on you. If they see that you are calm in the environment and that you are safe there, they will learn to trust that they are in a place of safety, too.

It is always a good idea to spend the whole of the first day with your bird. You don't have to interact. However, it is good if the bird has an opportunity to watch you all day. So, choose a day when you are likely to be home as the first day of your bird with you and your family.

2. Is it safe to introduce Lorikeets to other pets?

Choosing to allow your pets such as cats and dogs to interact with the birds or not is totally your call. Many Lorikeet owners vouch that they are able to train their cats and dogs to live with the Lorikeets successfully. However, in most cases, this only happens under supervision.

You have to understand that a cat or a dog is inherently a predator. That means they will always pose some amount of threat to your Lorikeet even after several years of interaction and living together. You may have seen pictures of birds and dogs or birds and cats playing with each other. This is certainly possible but it may not be worth the risk.

You may have a cat or a dog with the most wonderful personality. They could simply love to watch birds and may be quite gentle, too. However, do not forget that they do have certain instincts. And, in most cases, it may not even be the instinct. It is the sheer size and strength of the other animal that poses the threat. In case of cats, a lick or a bite can cause injuries and infections to the Lorikeet. Even your cat may take in bacteria and germs. In the case of a dog bite, it is usually fatal. This is because dogs have a higher bite strength that can just crush the Lorikeet.

This should not stop you from introducing your pets to one another. They need to be aware of each other's presence. To begin with, if you have a home with pets like cats and dogs, make sure that the cage you buy is very sturdy and has a lock that your pets or even the bird can't open easily. Never allow your pet, especially the cat, to perch on the cage. This makes the Lorikeet react in the same manner as it would to a predator in the wild and they may never form that bond.

Never keep them in separate rooms. Make sure that your bird cage is in a room where the cats or dogs or both normally rest. That way they will interact and get familiar with each other. You must maintain this interaction until you see that your dog or cat has no interest in the bird. They shouldn't care about the bird's movements and must show no signs of curiosity towards the bird. When you know that your pets are comfortable in the presence of the Lorikeet, you may try to take him out of the cage and bring him close to your pets. If your pets growl or snarl or try to lick the bird, stop them with a sharp, "NO!" That tells them that the bird is off limits.

The reason you need to keep them in the same room is so that you do not invite any surprises. In case you left the cage door open and your Lorikeet flew out, a dog or cat who is not familiar may attack him. However, if you have at least let them see each other constantly, the threat to your bird is less. In fact, some Lorikeet parents have only realized that it is safe to leave their Lorikeets and pets free and unattended by doing so accidentally. And, when they returned, they found that all the pets were in good health. But, never take this chance. Don't judge any pet by their personality first. This includes the birds. Remember always that they are creatures with a very strong predator instinct that can be triggered in any way. Keeping your Lorikeet in a safe cage when you are not around is the most recommended option.

3. Can Lorikeets be introduced to other birds?

Lorikeets are timid birds, no doubt. However, not all varieties of Lorikeets are compatible with one another. Some of them can get really aggressive when kept in a mixed aviary.

With respect to Lorikeets, a mixed aviary refers to different types of Lorikeets and not different species of birds entirely. The rule of thumb with Lorikeets is that they are best when kept with birds that are of the same physical structure as them. This includes canaries and other Lorikeets. Large birds like parrots or cockatoos may not be the best option if you want to house the birds together.

Compatibility among Lorikeets is best understood when you study the nature of the birds in the wild. If they are social birds that are not restricted to pairs, then they will most likely get along well. However, if these birds get too territorial during the breeding season, you may want to study a little more about them before you keep them together.

Lorikeets are usually categorized as pushy birds. This means that they can be kept in large aviaries with other birds like canaries as long as there is a good visual barrier between them. Lorikeets have the tendency to harass other birds unduly, making it very risky to have them together without these barriers.

It is best that you house your birds in pairs if you are going to keep them in a mixed aviary. You must at least ensure that there are equal numbers of male and female birds. That way the competition during the mating season will reduce, leading to less aggression.

If you already have an aviary or even a pet bird at home, the first thing you need to do is quarantine the new bird. You see, birds tend to be carriers of several diseases that can affect the whole flock. Even a seemingly healthy bird may develop health problems after the incubation period of these disease carrying microbes is completed.

The new bird must be kept in a separate cage in an entirely different room for at least 30 days. This is the incubation time of most of the parasites and microbes. If your bird shows any signs of illness within this period, you may return him to the pet store or the breeder if you have a valid health guarantee.

A health guarantee is normally provided for 90 days after the purchase of the bird. However, you need to make sure that the bird is checked by an avian vet within 72 hours of purchase.

The quarantining room should have a separate air source. This means, you can keep the new bird indoors if the other aviary is an outdoor one. It is best that you keep the new bird in a different room altogether. Some even recommend asking a friendly neighbor to keep your new bird for a few days.

Make sure you handle the birds that are already in your home before you handle the new bird. This includes feeding, changing water containers etc. If you do handle the new birds first, take a shower and change your clothes and shoes before you handle the existing birds.

During this time you may want to treat your new bird for parasites such as coccidian, giardia etc. Stool samples not more than 42 hours old should do the trick.

After quarantining, you can bring the cage of the new bird into the same room as the other birds. If the other birds are larger birds, it is best that you do not house them in the same enclosure. If they are Lorikeets or sparrows, you will have to observe the birds well before you place them together.

Once you keep the cages in the same room, observe the reaction of the other birds. Do they become irritable and aggressive? If yes, you may consider keeping them in separate enclosures. However, if the other birds merely respond to the calls of the new bird, which will make them noisier than usual, it may not be such a bad idea to introduce your birds.

You can introduce the birds by putting them in a neutral enclosure. That way, neither bird is territorial and aggressive. Individual interactions starting with the least aggressive bird is the best option.

Once all the birds in your aviary have been introduced to one another, you can try to place your new Lorikeets in the mixed aviary too. Even the slightest sign of aggression means that you need to get your new bird out and house him separately.

There are a few things that will help you decide if certain birds will be compatible or not. First, you need to understand the habitat of the bird. Birds that are comfortable feeding off the floor of the aviary will usually be less aggressive. On the other hand, if the bird species has special requirements with respect to the feeding area, the nesting spot, etc. they are aggressive.

These birds tend to hijack the nesting areas of other birds leading to a lot of confrontations and aggression among one another. If you do have such birds in your aviary which includes the java sparrow, diamond fire tail finch, cut throat finch, red brown finch or the crimson finch, it is best that you do not mix your birds.

When you house mixed birds in one cage, you are creating a colony. So, always ask your vet or breeder if a certain species is a colony bird or not. Lorikeets, for example, are successful colony birds. But, if you mix them with other species that aren't, you will be putting your birds at risk.

Even with successfully colonized birds, making sure that they get their individual space is mandatory. This means that each bird should have at least 2 cubic meters to himself. They also need to have their own perches and toys and also feeding containers that are easy to access and use. That way, you will have a peaceful colony of birds.

4. Why is my Lorikeet biting?

It is normal for a bird to become aggressive. They will bite and nip when they are displaying aggression. Now, it is possible that you have brought home a young female bird. A female that is hormonal will display a lot of territorial behavior. This behavior is aggravated when you provide a bed or a sleeping place in the cage. For a hormonal female, this becomes the possible nesting area and she will do everything she can to protect it.

If you have a female, you can deal with aggression by just putting a blanket over the cage at night to make her sleeping period comfortable. Remove any bed or resting area. You may also want to make small changes within the cage such as changing the toys or moving the bowls around. This will remove the concept of familiarity and your female bird will stop being so protective about her territory. You will do this even if it is a pair of Lorikeets with one male and one female.

If you have a male that is aggressive, the response to aggression is the key to controlling it. There is a good chance that your bird is biting to seek attention and not really to attack you. This means you have to avoid responses like screaming or a sudden "No!" That will only encourage the bird to continue to bite.

Look around the area that the birds are placed in. Mirrors and large toys should be removed to prevent aggression. In the case of males, they see it as a threat. On the other hand, female birds will think that a snuggly toy or even her own reflection is a possible mate. That will make her hormonal and tough to deal with.

5. Why is my Lorikeet screaming?

Lorikeet birds may scream at a certain time of the day. This is acceptable as it is their natural urge to call out to their flock at a certain time of the day. If your parrot, on the other hand, screams every time you leave the room, you have a problem on hand. You need to make sure that the bird understands that screaming is not the best way to get your attention.

You can do this by ignoring the bird when he screams and giving him attention only when he stops screaming. If you come running back to the room when you hear the bird scream he gets a message that this is what he needs to do in order to get your attention. If you come in and scold him in a loud voice, it is worse. He will think that you are responding to his calls. Instead, come in only when he stops shouting. That tells him that you will be close to him only when he behaves in an appropriate manner.

Whenever you leave the room, it is a good idea to put a few toys into your bird's cage. This teaches the bird that it is time for some fun when you are going out. He will become more independent that way and will stop screaming every time you left the room for even just a minute.

6. How to read the bird's body language?

Your Lorikeet will use body language to communicate with you. He will also use different types of calls that you need to learn to decipher when you are forming a bond with your Lorikeet. Let us talk about the vocalizations first and then go to the visual communication through the body.

Vocalization

Lorikeets are extremely vocal birds and will rely on their voices as an effective means of communication. There are some trademark sounds that your bird will make to tell you how he or she is feeling:

- **Talking, Whistling and Singing:** This means that your bird is happy and content

- **Chattering:** The most commonly used method to get your attention. This is seen in birds that are still learning to talk.

- **Clicking the tongue:** They are just having fun or are asking you to do something fun with them.

- **Low growl:** This is a sign of aggression and shows that something is troubling or threatening the Lorikeet. Look for objects that your bird dislikes and get it out of their sight. Never handle a growling Lorikeet.

Body Language

A Lorikeet will use his eyes, beak, head, wings, tail and feet to communicate with you. Here are some of the most commonly observed physical displays or visualizations in Lorikeets.

Beak

- Grinding the beak shows that your bird is satisfied and is ready for some rest.

- He will tug on your shirt collar with his beak indicating that he wants to get off or go back in the cage.

- He will lower his beak to the ground or floor of the cage to show you that he wants you to scratch him.

- This is a disgusting one but very endearing. A parrot will regurgitate in front of you as a sign of affection. In the wild, they regurgitate food so that they can share it with their mate!

Head:

- Bobbing the head up and down indicates that your pet is very happy or excited.

- If your Lorikeet lowers his head and turns it by 90 degrees, it means that he sees something that he wants.

- If he bobs his head and regurgitates, then you have been an excellent Lorikeet parent, congratulations!

Tail

- Wagging the tail is a sign of happiness and excitement. It means he wants to play with you.

- If the tail bobs up and down it is the sign of strenuous activity. This is how birds cool off. If tail bobbing occurs even when the bird is at rest, it is a sign of some illness.

- Tail fanning is the bird's attempt to look bigger and scare away a potential threat. It is a display of aggression.

Feet:

- If the Lorikeet paces up and down the cage or on the perch, he wants to come to you.

- If he stands fully straight, he wants to come you.

- If he scratches the floor of the cage, it means that he wants to get out of the cage. Do not give in to this behavior.

- Tapping the foot on the floor of the cage is yet another sign of aggression that you simply must not ignore.

Wings and feathers:

- Ruffled feathers show that the bird is unwell or cold.

- Quivering wings is a sign that the bird is ready to mate.

- Flapping the wings is an attempt at getting your attention.

- Flipping the wings on the other hand means that he is in pain or is agitated. If he also hunches his shoulders when he does this, he is deprived of attention or is really hungry.

- Drooping wings in older Lorikeets is a sign of some illness.

When you begin to understand the body language of your Lorikeets, you will be able to predict their behavior and eventually make your bond stronger. Once you are confident that your Lorikeet is not afraid of you, the next step is to start training him or her. This book will cover some of the basics. You have several resources such as online videos that will show you different tricks that you can try with your bird. The trick to all forms of training is the same. All you need to know is that with higher levels of difficulty, you need more patience.

7. Are Lorikeets trainable?

Training and taming your Lorikeet can take a good amount of patience. Some birds respond quickly to your training attempts while others will be slower. But, the fact that Lorikeets are very curious and playful makes it fun to train them. One very useful technique to train birds is the target point method. It is time consuming to get the bird initiated. However, once the birds are target trained, all the other things become really easy to teach.

Target training

Once you have built enough trust for the bird to eat from your hands, you can proceed to target training. You need to buy a clicker from any local pet store. Whenever you are going to offer the treat, just click once. If the sound alarms the bird, you can muffle it by holding the clicker inside your pocket or behind you. This tells your bird that whenever the clicker goes off, he will get a treat.

Then, you can start with the actual target training. You will need a stick, preferably a chopstick. When you hold it out to the bird through the cage and keep it still, the primary instinct of a Lorikeet is to approach it and chew at it. As soon as he does that click and give him a treat. Slowly draw the stick further away and see if the bird walks towards it. You should be able to guide the parrot around the cage using the target stick. You can even eliminate the treat. Just the stick will be motivation for the bird.

Note; If your parrot does not approach the stick the first time, touch the beak with the stick, click and offer the treat. Do this till the bird learns to approach the target stick.

Getting the parrot out of the cage
The target stick is a great aid to get your bird out of the cage. If you just keep the cage door open and wait for the bird to step out, it is probably never going to happen. You see, Lorikeets are extremely territorial and will not be motivated to get out of the cage so easily.

You can lead the bird out of the cage using the target stick a couple of times. Then, place some foraging toys around so that the bird finds some motivation to come out. Just hold the target stick at the entrance of the cage and keep pulling it away so that the bird follows it. When he is out of the cage, close the door and let him play with the toys offered to him.

Getting him back into the cage
One of the biggest challenges is putting the Lorikeet back in the cage. They will think of their time outside the cage as bonding time with you. When you put them back in the cage, they feel like you do not want to be with them anymore. Hence, they form a negative association with being put back. Then they will even resist coming out of the cage because they hate the idea of being put away.

You need to make sure that going back into the cage is viewed as a reward. When you put the bird back into the cage, make sure that there is a great meal waiting for the bird in the cage. That will make him excited to get back in.

Note: Teaching your Lorikeet to come out of the cage and go back in works best in the morning during feeding time. Take them out before feeding and put them back in after the bowls have been filled. That way, the hungry bird will look forward to getting back in.

Step up training

This is the most important thing to teach a Lorikeet. Especially when there is any emergency like a fire, your bird should trust you enough to step up on your finger.

You can do this after the bird has been taught to step out of the cage. Hold your finger in front of the open cage door horizontally. That way, the finger resembles a branch. Pointing your finger at the bird will make him bite as he thinks it is food.

Hold the finger steady and keep the target stick just behind the finger. In a soft voice, say "Step Up". The bird may step up instantly or may back away. Either way, give him a treat and try again. Eventually, when he does step on to your finger, give him a reward.

You need to make sure that your fingers are absolutely still when the bird steps up. If you move, he will lose trust immediately. Even if he puts his beak around your finger, hold it steady. He is only checking to see if your finger is a sturdy perch.

Slowly, the bird will just step up when you offer the finger. You can then use the target stick to lead him onto your shoulder or on your head.

Potty training

This will prevent any droppings around your home. It will give the Lorikeet a designated place to go and make a potty. This training is mandatory if you are letting your bird out of the cage often. Remember that Lorikeets poop every 15-20 minutes. So if they are not trained, your home will be a mess.

You need to establish with the bird that the best place to poop is his own cage. In the morning when you wake up, place a paper on the floor of the cage. Once the bird poops, give him a treat and shower him with praises.

Study the body language of the bird before pooping. He will normally crouch and lift the tail up. This knowledge will help you when you take the bird out of the cage. Whenever you take the bird out, watch for the signs of pooping. Then, place the paper in a box or a trash can and hold the bird over it. When he poops in the designated area, show him that you are very excited and happy and offer him a treat. The bird will learn that he can only poop over the box or trash can.

Will Lorikeets talk?

Unlike other parrots, Lorikeets will not learn to say full sentences. However, they are good at imitating sounds. Lorikeet owners claim that their birds will mimic sounds like doorbells, oven sounds or phone rings.

But, there are rare instances when they may even pick up a word like hi or hello. If you want your bird to say anything in particular, you will have to keep saying the word to him. When you say the word that you want him to learn, make sure that the space is free from any distractions, including toys. So, the best place would be outside the cage when your bird is perched upon your shoulder or finger. Saying the word in a high pitched, excited voice increases the chances of learning.

8.Is my Lorikeet jealous?

There is such a thing as over bonding which is actually the root cause of several behavioral problems, mainly jealousy. Proper training prevents over bonding and ensure that you have a well behave bird who is friendly and easy to handle.

What are the signs of bonding?

From the time you bring the bird into your home, you will notice that he slowly warms up to you and your family. Then, the bonding process progresses to a point when you are able to keep your bird on your shoulder and go about your daily activities. Let us take a look at the signs that show you that your bird is bonding with you.

Warming up: The Initial Stage

- Your parrot will stop other activity and watch you when you are in the room or when you are passing by the cage. He will not be scared or nervous, however.

- He will follow your movements and will respond to your talking with different vocalizations. In case of the Lorikeet, he may just repeat the words that you say.

- The bird moves towards you when you approach the cage.

- When you offer food from your hand, the bird eats it calmly.

The Progression: After the bird is "Hand tamed"
- He will step up on to your finger and will also let you pet him.

- He will call out to you when you are not around and he misses you.

- He may climb on your hand or shoulder, even when you do not ask him to.

The bond: Your bird loves you
- He will preen and groom your hair. Even if that means he is just making it messier.

- He will not resist grooming activities like bathing or wing clipping. He will even let you hold him in awkward positions such as being upside down.

- He begins to trust you completely and even displays mating behavior such as regurgitation of food when you are around.

Signs of over-bonding

- The bird becomes very angry and aggressive when you talk to anyone else, especially another bird. He will scream and will even tear his toys apart.

- He is only happy if you are around and will always groom your hair or will try to feed you and display courting behavior. When you are gone, he will scream, become very scared or will just be depressed.

- The bird will not allow anyone else to handle him or touch him except the person he has bonded with.

- If any other person receives a slight bit of attention from the one he has bonded with, he will attack and bite them.
- The bird is extremely defensive about the person he is bonded with. If anyone tries to even touch the human he has bonded with, he will bite them. He will also attack other pets around your home.

- He will not let anyone else feed him.

Having an over-bonded parrot can be very difficult. You will not be able to travel and leave the bird in someone else's care. He is also a potential threat to everyone around your home, especially children. The only way to prevent over-bonding is properly training your bird and socializing him. This is not a difficult thing to do with Lorikeets.

9.Is my Lorikeet scared?

It is very normal for birds to display fear for the first few days. They are trying to get accustomed to a new environment. That can be really overwhelming. They have to deal with the sights and sounds in your home that are totally new and alien to them.

You will know that your Lorikeet is scared if you see him or her hiding his beak in his feathers, picking his feathers constantly or bites at something constantly. They will also have a flared ness as a sign of fear. If you have adopted a Lorikeet, it is possible that he or she has had really bad experiences with the previous owner and will take longer than expected to trust you. Give the bird time in such cases.

Make sure that your Lorikeet does not have to deal with any surprises. As we mentioned above, avoid any new faces for the first few days. If the bird is feeling threatened by any object in the room take it away. Keep your bird in an environment that is calm and quiet. There must be enough sunlight in the room as well.

If you feel like the fear is causing any behavioral problem like screaming or nipping, just let the bird be. The more you try to tame him when he is in this condition, the less likely he is to learn and adapt. Be observant towards the situations that arouse this behavior in the birds. Does he get scared when you try to pick him up? Is he afraid when children are around? Does he fear feeding time? There are several traumatic experiences that these birds keep in their mind. They will display overanxious traits only when these triggers are present. If you are unsure, you may consult an avian vet.

The last thing to remember with a Lorikeet who is scared is to never tower over him. Always stay at his eye level. The former behavior can increase fear and lead to aggression as well. Then, the bird will think of you as a predator and it will become particularly hard to build trust with such a bird.

When the bird looks at your movements regularly and sees that you are only approaching him to feed and clean, he will eventually learn that you mean no harm. He will begin to lose fear and will show it by approaching you when you are near the cage. This is when you can start all your bonding process with your Lorikeet.

The thumb rule with fear or aggression is to never overwhelm the bird. Make sure that you tell your family members to allow the bird to settle in before they try to bond or play with it. Stress can lead to poor eating habits, poor metabolism and severe illnesses in the bird. So, make sure that you are patient and don't misinterpret the behavior of the bird. You need to have patience and help the bird into your family one step at a time.

After three days, when you see that the bird is settling in, you need to start gaining its trust. There are two possibilities when you approach a parrot cage. First, the bird may be extremely comfortable and used to your presence. Second, he will display great discomfort by thrashing around inside the cage and even screaming. In case the bird is quiet, you can proceed to the next step and start giving him or her treats from your hands through the bars of the cage.

However, if your bird is really uncomfortable upon seeing you, you have to train him to stop doing that first. For this, approach the bird cage close enough to make him display the uncomfortable behavior. Then, do not go further or retreat. Just stand there until the bird calms down and then turn around and walk away. Do this a couple of times to tell your bird that if he wants you to leave or not get close to him, it will only happen if he is calm. Eventually, step closer and closer to the cage till you are close enough to touch it.

All breeds of parrots love the same treats, including Lorikeets. You can try almonds, seeds and even some varieties of fruits. In case your bird is not familiar with these treats, you can ask your breeder what to give the bird. You can also allow your bird to get used to these treats. That may take a little longer but it will make your job much easier in the long run.

To begin with, slowly place the food through the cage with your fingers. At first, your bird may not even eat what you offer. Then, once they realize that you are offering a treat, they may consider eating straight out of your fingers. When they are comfortable doing this, you can do the next thing which is opening the cage door and slowly offer the treat on your palm.

Chapter 5) Breeding Lorikeets

Some Lorikeet breeders will tell you that they breed all year around. That is not quite true. The most prominent breeding season for Lorikeets is when the temperature increases and the sunlight increases, which is typically in spring. Some of them may even become hormonal in summer. If you have a pair of Lorikeets- a male and a female, you need to know that they might mate and that you may have to be prepared to raise the babies and take care of the brooding female. The usual age of maturity for Lorikeets is about 2 years.

1.Will your Lorikeets mate?

Just having a pair of Lorikeets (one male and one female) does not guarantee that they will mate. Lorikeets are monogamous birds. This means that they will only mate with one partner in a lifetime. So, for the Suns to breed, they need to like each other. If you see favorable behavior such as preening the feathers of each other, sleeping next to each other, locking beaks almost like they are kissing and just staying together all the time, you can safely say that you have a nuptial bond between the birds. A sign that these birds are mates is feeding each other. They are likely to mate in the breeding season.

To encourage breeding, you need to watch their behavior closely. If you notice the male mounting the female, you need to ensure that they get some peace and quiet. Lorikeets will not breed if there is any interference such as noise from television, human voices or any disturbance from the pets. You can change their current enclosure to a special nesting cage that is placed in a quiet room. Remember, Lorikeets will not show specific breeding or mating behavior like other birds. This is true for most birds from the Lorikeet family.

2.Setting up for Breeding Season

Lorikeets are shy birds and will need a specific nesting box if they need to be encouraged to breed. You need to get a large nesting box that is at least 18 inches deep or more. This is basically to make sure that the nesting material, usually something soft like pine shavings, is available in plenty. Lorikeets tend to keep kicking this material out and if the nest is not deep enough, there are chances that the amount of pine shavings available will not be enough when the eggs are laid.

You can use a wooden nesting box. However, Lorikeets tend to be chewers and may damage the box. So a metal one is more suitable. The idea is to have a nesting box that can last for several breeding seasons. You see, Lorikeets prefer the same nesting box year after year.

This box can be placed at a high position in the cage. If you have a special nesting cage, you can place it there. Remember that height is an important factor for brooding hens to feel comfortable.

In case your bird does not have enough access to light, you may have to set up infrared lighting that you need to turn on at about 4 pm and turn off by about 10 pm. You need not increase temperatures in case of Lorikeets.

3.Signs of Egg Laying

You should watch your Lorikeet's behavior closely to make sure that you know when she may lay eggs. You will see some obvious signs like eating more from the mineral block or chewing from the cuttlebone. She will also become very cranky and noisy. She becomes very territorial and is a little aggressive as well. She will start seeking your attention and will want you to accept annoying behavior such as nipping at your shirt or biting. Do not encourage that. She will also develop a bald patch on the belly which is called the brood patch. This is to help her pass heat from her body to the eggs.

When she is ready, she will lay the egg in the nesting box and will incubate it for about 28 days when provided with nesting conditions such as toys, sunlight and a lot of attention. Some Lorikeet owners will just leave their pet alone as soon as the eggs are laid. This makes the female actually lose interest in the eggs. They believe that you do not care about them because of the eggs. This kind of behavior is displayed when the Lorikeet owners do not want the eggs to hatch.

Each clutch will have between 1 to 5 eggs. The hen lays one egg each day. It is possible that the first clutch is infertile. The larger the species of Lorikeet, the larger the size of the clutch.

If your Lorikeet loses interest in the eggs for other reasons and you do not want the eggs to be damaged, you can bring home an incubator. This is an expensive piece of equipment.

4.Raising the Baby Lorikeets

Raising the chicks is a lot of responsibility. Most often, pet owners just let the Lorikeet pair to raise their hatchlings who will arrive after about 28 days of incubation. The parents will feed the babies for 8 weeks and really care for them. Now, you have three options when it comes to rearing the baby Lorikeets:

With the Parents
Lorikeet chicks grow really fast. If you do not disturb the hatchlings and just leave them in the box, then the parents will raise them. At about 4 weeks, these babies will develop pin feathers. When they are 8 weeks old, they are fully weaned at the age of 8 weeks.

If you interfere ever so slightly with the parents, you will have to take up the responsibility of raising the chicks. This is a lot of work and definitely not for someone who has no experience. You can watch as the parents feed and tame their young just like in the wild and it is a fascinating sight. Allowing the hatchlings to be hand raised has several advantages. To begin with, it is more economical. Second, these birds are likely to make better breeding specimens.

Hand Raising the Chicks
Some Lorikeet owners may want to hand raise the chicks to build a good bond with them. It is also true that these baby birds make amazing pets. You must not take the baby out of the nest immediately after hatching. It is a good idea to leave them there until they are at least 4 weeks old. These babies will believe that they are human beings when they are raised by people. They will start to preen your hair, cuddle up towards you and even give you gentle nips or kisses.

The older the chicks are when they are removed from the nest, the stronger they are. This makes them easier to handle and less susceptible to infections. Once they are out you need to start hand feeding them. Now, there are special mixes called hand rearing formula that you can buy in any pet store. These formulae are rich in nutrients and will help the babies grow healthy.

Follow the directions for heating as mentioned on the box. The chicks need their food to be at a certain temperature in order to process them properly. You also need to feed them the number of times recommended on the box. There are at least 3-4 feeding cycles in a day, separated by a few hours.

Co -parenting
You may also choose to work with the Lorikeet parents and raise the chicks with them. This means that the Lorikeet parents will also be a part

of the raising process. You will take turns between the feeding cycles and the babies will be removed from the nest to hand feed at least once a day.

Co-parenting is only possible when you have a very trusting relationship with your birds. If they can accept your attempts to take the babies out as assistance and not acceptance, then you can do this. Your birds need to be extremely calm to allow you to co-parent the chicks. Otherwise they will develop aggressive behavior which they will direct at each other. The male may attack the female or they may even kill the hatchlings. You must back off if the birds show any signs of resistance.

However, if the birds accept your assistance, it can be a wonderfully rewarding experience for you. The responsibility is reduced on your part and on the part of the Lorikeet parents, the babies are more social and tame and the parents still have the pleasure raising their own young.

It does not matter how you choose to raise the birds. Remember that all the experiences are equally rewarding. You may choose to add these birds to your flock. That is, however, not a practical thing to do as Lorikeets that have mated once will do so every year and the babies have a life span of 30 years or more. So, it is a good idea to find these babies loving homes when they are a few years old.

In case you find the first experience with the chicks very taxing, you can discourage breeding by disallowing ideal nesting conditions as mentioned above. Some pet Lorikeet owners also avoid raising chicks because they find it very hard to part with them.

Chapter 6) Travelling with Lorikeets

Travelling can become a challenge with Lorikeets. You can take your bird along in some cases. Of course, if you decide to move, you will have to figure out a way to take your bird with you or find a foster home for the bird.

In case of temporary travel, however, it is advised that you keep the bird at home under the care of a pet sitter or a friend or neighbor. Travelling can be quite stressful for your bird.

However, there are some circumstances that you cannot avoid, such as going to the vet. In these case, you will have to ensure that your Lorikeet is comfortable enough to at least travel by car.

1.Driving with your Lorikeet

It is recommended that you get a separate travelling cage for your Lorikeet. This is a smaller cage that is easier to carry around. Make the Lorikeet like this cage by adding toys and perches and leading him into it occasionally with some treats. That way, he knows that it is a safe place to be in. He also need to feel like it is a positive place to be in.

The next step is to introduce your Lorikeet to car drives. If you know that you may have to take the bird on long car journeys, either to visit the vet or because of an impending move, you need to prepare him for this.

The Drive

First transfer your Lorikeet to the travel cage. Then place the cage in the car. Before you do this, ensure that the temperature of the car is at room level. You may have to turn the heat up or down depending on the season. Too much heat can cause heat strokes and too much cold will stress the bird unnecessarily.

Leave the cage in the car for a few minutes and take him back home. Spend a week to just get him accustomed to sitting in your car comfortably. He should display very normal behavior and must not seem perturbed. Then, you can move to the next step which is the actual drive.

For the drive, place the cage in the back seat and strap it in place with the seat belt. Take a small drive down the block and see how the bird reacts. If he is whistling and normal, you have a bird who likes to travel. On the other hand if he gets distressed and sits in a corner of the cage, shivers or vomits, it means that you need to be more persistent.

You need to make the idea of coming into a car fun for the bird. That includes talking to him when you are driving, praising him for staying calm and offering him a lot of juicy fruits like pineapples that are not just tasty but also hydrating for your bird. Eventually, your bird will start accepting the car as a neutral and fun space. Then you can increase the length of the drives. For long drives, makes sure that you have enough substrate on the floor, plenty of access to fresh water and some treats that he enjoys.

If you have to move houses

When you are moving, you will have several bags in your car while you are driving. This is also stressful for a Lorikeet. So, you need to add one bag at a time and continue to take him on drives. You need to do this till you are able to place all the bags in the car along with the bird cage and drive without stressing the bird.

The reason you need to add the bags one at a time and really plan for a move is that the color, shape and size of the bag can be scary for the birds. If you can plan well, you will be able keep the stress levels low not just for the bird but for yourself too.

When you are ready to move, make an appointment with your avian vet for a final examination that renders your Lorikeet fit to travel. Make sure you get all the medical records of your Lorikeet from your vet to be able to share it with the new one.

Housebreaking into a new home will not be as stressful for your bird because you are around. Still, give them time and appreciate their need to be left alone and soak in the new environment.

2.Finding a Sitter

You may want to travel to a different state or country with your Lorikeet. This is a big step if you are moving out as you will have to check the laws regarding brining the bird into another country. Some countries have very strict quarantining measures. So if you are planning a move, you need to make sure that your Lorikeet will be able to come with you. If not, you have to change your option of travel or you may have to take the hard way out by finding a new home for your Sun.

But, if you are only travelling temporarily on a vacation or for a business trip, taking your bird along is not recommended. It is a better idea to leave him in a place that is more familiar to him. This can be under the care of a relative, a pet sitter or even in a facility that may be provided by your own avian vet. For a temporary trip, it is not really worth putting your Lorikeet through so much stress.

Finding someone to care for your Lorikeet

The best option is to keep your Lorikeet in your home and request your friend or relative to take care of the bird. They should be entirely trust worthy. This is the best and most reliable option. However, if you do not have someone you know who can take care of your bird, you can always hire a pet sitter.

There are several professional pet sitters who can follow your routine and exact care while you are away. You can look up the yellow pages, ask fellow bird owners or check the internet for options. Two of the most reliable sources to find pet sitters for your Lorikeet are National Association of Pet Sitters or www.petsitters.org and Pet Sitters International or www.petsit.com.

As per the National Association of Professional Pet Sitters, here are a few guidelines that you can follow to find a good pet sitter:

- Look for a sitter who has some commercial liability insurance. These are bonded sitters who can be held responsible in case something goes wrong with your pet.

- Make sure you have enough references from past clients. You can also ask the sitter to connect you with them. If there is any hesitation, you may want to reconsider.

- You need to get a complete written description of all the services that they will provide including the fees.

- You need to meet the pet sitter once. Ask them to visit your home and discuss all the services in complete detail.

- Be observant when you are interviewing the sitter. Is he comfortable with your Lorikeet? Ask him if he owns birds and also about the experience that he has with sitting birds.

- You need to make a written contract in case you decide to use the services of a particular sitter. The most important thing is to check for his or her arrangements with veterinarians. In case your bird falls sick or there is any emergency find out how he or she is going to deal with it.

- If the sitter herself or himself falls sick and is unable to care for your bird, is there any replacement. If so, meet that person.

In case you are not comfortable with the idea of leaving the bird with a sitter, there are several boarding options. The best one is with your avian vet if they provide those services. If not, you can ask them to recommend a suitable boarding for your pet Lorikeet. Make sure you check the conditions of boarding and that your bird will be safe from any infections during this time.

3.Air Travel with Lorikeets

In case you have to take your bird on a plane for whatever reasons, it is a process that you have to plan very carefully. If not done properly, you could be putting the health of your bird at risk.

Know the laws

There are several wildlife laws in order to protect certain species of animals. Now, as you know Lorikeets are considered endangered and there may be several laws that make it hard for you to take the bird out of your country or even out of your state. There are three laws that you need to thoroughly check before you make any overseas plans involving the Lorikeet:

1. Convention on the International Trade in Endangered Species of Wild Fauna and Flora (CITES)
2. Wild Bird Conservation Act
3. Endangered Species Act

These laws have been enforced to ensure that these birds are safe and not illegally transported or traded. You can check the websites of these laws to see what laws are in reference with your Lorikeet. You may even take the assistance of your Avian vet in determining whether travel to certain countries is possible with Lorikeets or not. You may have to apply for special permits that will allow you to travel with your Pet Lorikeet. It can take up to 60 days to process these permits. So, you need to plan well in advance. You have to check these laws even if you are only crossing state borders.

Once this is done, the next step is the actual plane travel which can be a traumatic experience for your Lorikeet. Here are some things that you need to do to make sure that air travel is hassle free:

- Talk to different airlines and understand their regulations about transporting pets. Now, with birds, the airlines will have specifications about how long the bird can stay in cargo. If your flight is longer than the time given, you may have to break your trip down to various transits. If switching planes is necessary, make sure you do not have to switch the airlines. This means you have to learn a whole new set of rules.

- Then, get a carrier as per the guidelines of the airlines.
- 10 days prior to the air travel, you need to get a health certificate from your avian vet. If you are travelling overseas, you will have to get this certificate signed by the USDA and the Animal and Plant Health Inspection Service.

- You need to take a CITES permit with you when travelling overseas.

- Make sure that your bird is strapped and harnessed in case his wings have not been clipped. In case of long flights, it is recommended that you have the bird's wings trimmed.

- You must carry enough food supplies with you for the whole trip. In the travelling cage, make sure you have enough food available to the bird. You can also get a water dropper to keep the bird hydrated. Substrate should be increased to make the flight comfortable for your bird.

After you have all this in place, you can travel with your Lorikeet. Remember that it may take a little settling in after flight journeys. These journeys are extremely stressful for the bird and can make them anxious. If you notice any unusual behavior in your Lorikeet, make sure that you have him checked by an avian vet the moment you are able to. There may be stress related problems or even breathing issues that your bird may develop on long flights.

Make sure that you are gentle with your Lorikeet and that you let him know that you really appreciate his cooperation during the flight. You cannot take pets in cabins as you would know. So always thoroughly check the airlines policies and even ask fellow bird owners about their experiences with different airline and choose one that you can truly trust. After all, you do not want him to be dumped in the back of the cargo like baggage. He should be able to travel comfortably at the very least and airline personnel should handle your pet Lorikeet with lots of care.

Chapter 7) Lorikeet Health

Keeping your Lorikeet healthy is your first priority. These birds, like any other species of birds are susceptible to several health issues. Making sure that you are able to identify these health issues can prevent the worst. Remember, birds are very good at hiding their illnesses. This is a way of staying safe in the wild to ensure that predators don't think that they are vulnerable.

This chapter tells you about the different health issues with Lorikeets, how to identify them and how to prevent them.

1.Identifying a sick bird

There are several symptoms that help you identify a sick bird. These symptoms can either be mild or intense. In any case, you have to be alert and identify the slightest change or deviation from normal. That can work wonders in saving your bird's life.

Here are a few symptoms that can help you identify illnesses in your birds and provide timely assistance:

- **Fluffed feathers**
  If your bird looks fluffy or puffed up in appearance, it is the most obvious sign of an ill bird. The common reason for fluffing up feathers is to keep himself warm.

  When your bird tries to do this, you will see that the regular sleek frame is lost. The bird will actually look fat and extremely messy. Sometimes, birds may just puff up their feathers for some time while preening. But if the puffiness is prolonged, it is a matter of great concern.

  However, puffiness must never be ignored even if the bird retracts the feathers when you approach him. This is a common defense mechanism as the bird does not look vulnerable. You must also be observant of the bird's body language. If the bird looks sick or you have the slightest suspicion, you need to make sure that you pay attention.

- **Wet vent**

  If the vent area of the bird is constantly vet, then it can be considered a symptom of illness. This is the underside of the bird where the bird excretes from. If the bird is healthy, the vent is dry and clean.

- **Respiratory issues**

  One of the most common tell gate signs of sickness in a bird is abnormal or heavy breathing. This type of breathing without any physical exertion means that the bird may be unwell. In addition to heavy breathing the bird will also exhibit tail bobbing.

  If the bird is sneezing, coughing or has some sort of nasal discharge, it is an indication of illness. Hold the bird close to you if you have any suspicion. You may be able to hear a distinct clicking sound which indicates chances of mites or parasites in the air sac. This needs to be checked immediately to help the bird recover at the earliest.

- **Inactivity**

  Lorikeets are usually quite active and love to fly about or just interact with one another. If your bird is sleepy all the time and is found catching untimely naps, it is a warning sign.

  Birds will nap in the afternoons or during the day. However, they seldom nap when the rest of their cage mates are active. If your bird is snoozing while the others are active, you need to look at it as a warning sign.

  Birds that sit at the bottom of the cage for long hours may also be unwell. This is not a common thing especially in an aviary as Lorikeets prefer to interact with one another and will seldom be isolated in this manner. If they have the habit of sitting on the floor of the cage, it will usually be with their partners.

  However, if you see that your Lorikeets are shunning the company of other birds, especially their own partners, you need to understand that there is definitely some problem with the bird.

- **Loss of appetite**

  If a bird loses interest in food because of any illness, it is a sign of great concern. Always be observant of your birds. The thing with Lorikeets is that they do not want to appear unwell or sick. They may just pretend to eat the food you have given to them to make sure that they do not look vulnerable. However, they could only be sifting through the food and may not be actually consuming anything.

- **Lack of singing**
Vocalization is the most important sign of health especially in flinches. These birds are known for their unique songs and vocalization patterns.

When birds are unwell they remain unusually silent. The idea behind this is to make sure that they do not attract any unwanted attention from predators.

In addition to this, birds that are unwell will also do this as a method of saving up on their energy. If a bird who normally loves to chirp and sing becomes abnormally silent, you must immediately take him to your vet.

- **Unusual droppings**
Whenever you are cleaning out the substrate of the cage, make sure that you check the droppings of the birds. If the droppings are abnormal or have some unusual color, it could be a sign of indigestion or some disease.

If you have several birds in your aviary that belong to different families and species, this can be a little challenging. However, you can watch out for a few basic things such as the urates which should be white and dry in color. On the other hand if it dries up to look green or yellow, you need to show some concern immediately.
Maintenance of Lorikeets depends mostly on simple observation. In case you are unable to spend time watching your birds, you will never become familiar with the regular and normal behavior. As a result, you will also be unable to identify anything out of the ordinary.

In fact, you may miss out on initial symptoms of diseases that can be managed fairly easily. Even if you stop paying attention for a short time, you can miss out on some important behavioral changes that can be pivotal in saving the bird's life.

One thing all bird owners should know about is that birds prefer to hide their illness in order to look fit. In most cases, by the time the symptom becomes obvious, the bird is already very sick.

If you have an aviary, a sick bird is not only a matter of concern because of his health. He is a ticking time bomb that can affect the rest of the flock in no time.

If you are observant and find the symptoms early, you can have the bird quarantined and ensure that the rest of your flock is safe too. You have to first identify that your bird is sick. The next step is to narrow in on which disease it actually is. Lastly, you need to take all the preventive measures necessary for your aviary in order to keep the birds healthy.

2.Common illnesses in Lorikeets

Like all species of birds, the Lorikeet is also susceptible to attack and infection by certain microbes. These birds are genetically predisposed to certain conditions and you need to make sure that you take care accordingly.

There are other factors like nutrition and hygiene that also affect the health of your bird to a large extent.

a.Nutritional diseases

As discussed before, the metabolism in Lorikeets is very high. As a result, their body also demands a lot of nutrients. Birds are quicker than any other creature in the animal kingdom to depict the signs of malnutrition as well.

In many cases, pet birds have been diagnosed with nutritional diseases more often. In most cases, the immunity of the bird towards disease causing organisms is compromised when his nutritional requirements are not met.

It is very common to see birds showcase nutritional problems when they are in the breeding cycle. Problems like calcium deficiency are most prevalent in these birds. This leads to a lot of complications like egg binding or prolapse of the oviduct.

Each species has a different type of response to deficits in nutrition. In case of the Lorikeets, you will see a lot of tell gate signs. The most common nutritional diseases in Lorikeets include:

Obesity

This is the most common nutritional disorder, often ending in hepatic lipidosis or fatty liver. This condition has been observed in birds that are usually on a high fat seed only diet. This type of diet also leads to other issues like lowered calcium in the blood. Seeds also lack nutrients like vitamin A.

Two organs of the bird's body that are normally affected by obesity are the liver and the heart. Over time, all the fat that has been accumulated in the blood is passed on into the liver. This leads to a drastic decrease in the amount of functional tissue in the liver.

This condition also makes the liver very enlarged. If the fat accumulation occurs around the heart of the bird, the normal functioning of the heart is also compromised.

If the bird is overweight, he is not able to perform simple tasks such as flying or bathing in the water trough.

Symptoms of hepatic lipidosis

- The fat deposits are seen on the abdomen and chest, making these areas look large and buxom.

- The beak tends to grow rather abnormally. This condition is often identified by those who groom the bird and trim the beak at the vet's office.

- You will see obvious black spots on the toenails and the beak. This is primarily because the functionality of the liver is compromised. The clotting of blood does not occur properly leading to bruise like splotches on the beak and the nails.

- The liver is enlarged. Of course, this is not seen visually. When the bird is being checked by the vet, this becomes obvious. In smaller birds like Lorikeets, you can see this enlarged liver through the screen if you just moisten the skin with some alcohol.

These clinical signs are noticed in birds of all species. If you do not curb the fat intake of your bird, the regular bodily functions are largely compromised. Even simple stress like a loud noise can be too stressful for the bird leading to death.

Diagnosis

- Physical examinations are the first step to diagnosis.

- Your vet may also require the blood to be tested for anemia, lipemia or chances of jaundiced plasma which indicate compromised functioning of the liver.

Treatment

The best way to manage this condition is by improving the nutrition of your bird. You can prevent this condition entirely if you are careful about what you are feeding the bird.

Make sure that your bird gets a good balance of homemade food as well as commercially available food for the best possible results.

Some medicines such as probenecid or colchicine can be administered to help birds who have been severely affected.

Hypovitaminosis A

This is yet another condition that you will see in birds that have been maintained on an all seed diet. Most seeds and nuts do not have any traces of vitamin A.

The mucous membrane and the epithelial tissue is maintained by Vitamin A. When the levels of this nutrient drop, resistance to pathogenic or disease causing organisms also decreases.

You will commonly notice infections of the sinus and the respiratory tract in birds that have a deficiency of Vitamin A. you will also notice scaliness, flakiness and thickening of the skin of the bird's feet.

Symptoms of Vitamin A deficiency

- White plaques are seen on the roof of the mouth.

- A change in the functionality of the tear glands and the salivary glands leads to high levels of oral mucous.

- Respiratory difficulty accompanied by problems like coughing are quite common in birds with this condition.

- When the lack of vitamin A leads to compromised immunity, it manifests in the form of abscesses in the respiratory tract, the crop and the oral cavity of the bird.

- In case of brightly colored birds such as Lorikeets, the coloration of the plumage will also fade away with time.

- The hatchability rate of the clutches will decrease quite drastically.

- The chicks that do hatch may not survive or may fail to gain wait and die eventually.

Treatment

Preventive measures such as a healthy diet and proper supplementation are the best options for your bird. In case your bird develops this condition despite all the care, here are a few things that you can try:

- Provide commercial feed that is fortified with Vitamin A. These foods are often given along with water.

- The amount of orange and red vegetables as well as green leafy vegetables should be increased in your bird's diet.

- You can provide your bird with beta- carotene supplements. In most clinical cases this supplement is injected.

- Add a few drops of the extracts from a Vitamin A gel capsule into your bird's food.

- Cod liver oil can be added to your bird's diet. This is also quite easy to mix with dry foods like pellets and seeds.

With a balanced vitamin A intake, you will notice that your birds become more and more resistant to common health issues. You will also notice a very positive change in the reproductive cycle and results with regular Vitamin A supplements.

Hypervitaminosis A

Just as the deficiency of nutrients can lead to a lot of health problems, an excess of the same nutrient can be toxic to the bird. Many bird owners tend to over-supplement the diet of their birds leading to several complications.

The only sad thing is that this is a poorly documented condition among birds. In case of other animals, it has been seen that an excess of vitamin A in the body, leads to a lot of fatigue and weakness in the bird. It can also lead to pain in the bones.

Calcium. Vitamin D3 and Phosphorous imbalance
If the diet of your bird consists mainly of oily seeds and grains, you will notice these imbalances. These foods have a very low ratio of phosphorous to calcium and are also deficient in Vitamin D3. Additionally, the calcium that is available to the bird is bound within the body in the form of soaps when the diet is too oily.

Calcium is one of the most important minerals as far as the birds are concerned. The production of the egg is highly hampered when the calcium intake is not good enough. Calcium is also required by the skeleton of the bird. If calcium and phosphorous are not absorbed properly, it can lead to bones that are underdeveloped or extremely fragile.

There are several other body functions such as the transmission of nerve impulses, muscle contractions and also metabolic processes that are affected by the calcium levels in the body.

Calcium metabolism is affected by the amount of Vitamin D3 and phosphorous in the bird's body. Therefore, providing only calcium is meaningless as it will not be utilized properly.

Ideally, the ration of calcium to phosphorous should be 2:1 in the body of birds like Lorikeets. This value can have a 0.5 variation and not more.

Symptoms of calcium, vitamin D3 and phosphorous imbalance

- Adult birds are highly uncoordinated in muscle function when there is an imbalance.
- Weakness is commonly seen in birds with this nutritional deficiency.
- Egg binding as well as paresis or fatigue is seen in egg laying birds that do not have enough calcium available in their diet.
- In case of chicks you will see that deformities in the bone and joint are very common.
- Spay leg formation is seen in birds that have less calcium intake.
Treatment

Supplementation is the best option when your bird has calcium deficiency. However, you need to be very careful when you are giving these supplements to your birds.
If not done properly, excessive amounts of phosphorous and calcium can lead to other complications.

If the level of calcium is beyond the necessary amount, it can lead to mineralization of the kidney and kidney failure. When calcium is available in large amounts, the absorption of essential trace elements like zinc and manganese is affected.

If the level of phosphorous is too high, it is seen that calcium is not absorbed properly. This is because any calcium in the body will be bound in the form of calcium phosphate that is not soluble. As a result, blood calcium level will be low.

You need to make sure that you do not provide any unwanted supplements if the natural foods are able to provide your bird with all the nutrients that he requires.

Imbalance in Vitamin D
The main function of Vitamin D is to make sure that calcium metabolism occurs in the body of the bird. Vitamin D can be equally problematic if the levels are either too low or too high.

If the diet of the bird consists of an excessive amount of Vitamin D, it leads to toxicosis which means that the amount of calcium absorbed by the body also increases drastically. In the initials stages, this is not an issue as the kidney is able to excrete the excess calcium out.

But with repetitive calcium excess, the function of the kidney is compromised leading to a reduced rate of glomerular filtration. As a result kidney stones are formed and can be extremely painful for your birds.
There are several factors such as the form of Vitamin D ingested, the amount of calcium and vitamin A in the diet etc. that determine the chances of toxicosis. The health of the kidney us another major factor.

For example, providing cholecalciferol vitamin D supplements are more toxic than supplements like ergocalciferol. In fact, the former puts the bird at 10 times more risk than the latter.

If your bird is being over-supplemented with vitamin D, there are chances that the kidney gets mineralized along with calcification of the blood. If you have fed your bird toxic amounts of Vitamin D3, you may balance it out by reducing calcium in the diet.

In case your bird has any nutritional imbalance, the best thing to do would be to provide the bird with a diet that is nutritionally adequate. Getting them on homemade food is the best option. Of course, you also have the option of providing them with recommended commercial foods.

Mineral sources like calcium carbonate that can be found in egg or oyster shells are ideal for Lorikeets. You can also give your bird natural sources like milk, yoghurt, cheese, spinach and broccoli. If you are giving your bird eggs, make sure that it is not raw to reduce any risk of salmonellosis.

Deficiency of iodine
A seed based diet is usually responsible for iodine deficiency in the body. Thyroxine which is responsible for thyroid gland function is not formed in the body without adequate amounts of iodine.

It is necessary to give your bird iodine supplements if you are keeping them on a seed only diet. This supplement can be added into the food or water of the bird

Goiter is the result of iodine deficiency. The thyroid gland is present in the area where the trachea branches out into the lungs. This is just above the heart. As a result, when these glands become enlarged, a lot of pressure is applied on the voice box and the trachea. You will notice that birds have great difficulty breathing when they suffer from iodine deficiency for this very reason.

You will notice a wheeze, click or a squeaking sound whenever your bird tries to breathe. You will also notice vomiting in birds that have an iodine deficiency.

Goiter develops very slowly but gets very bad progressively. The larger the thyroid gets, the more obvious the sounds while breathing become. In many cases, the bird needs to exert himself physically and hold his head up in order to breathe.

There is always a chance of secondary bacterial invasion or fungal infection. This condition also leads to weight gain, deposits of fat on the internal organs, compromised feather quality and a lot of other secondary issues.

Although this is a rare deficiency in Lorikeets, you need to be watchful. The treatment of the condition is determined by the severity of deficiency.

Treatment of iodine deficiency

- In case of a mild deficiency, adding iodine supplements in the food or water can help.

- In extreme cases, your bird may have to be hospitalized to receive sodium iodide injections daily until this condition is reversed.

- Preventive measures are important following the treatment in the form of good diet and necessary supplements.

Hemochromatosis
Iron storage disease or hemochromatosis is very common in nectar eating birds like flinches and is the result of the bird's inability to excrete any excessive iron. This leads to damage in the heart, kidneys and the liver. Blood breakdown and chronic stress can be caused by hemochromatosis.

Several enzymes are not formed when there is an excess of iron in the body. In addition to that it also leads to genetic predisposition of the hatchlings to this condition.

You will notice difficulty in breathing along with a distension of the abdomen. Discolored droppings are common with birds who have hemochromatosis.

Treatment of hemochromatosis

- Long term phlebotomies or blood-letting are carried out in a weekly basis in order to reduce the iron deposits.

- The iron levels in blood serum are constantly monitored to ensure that they do not exceed 150mg.

- A hematocrit or CBC is used to make sure that the bird recovers from these blood-letting sessions.

- A medicine called deferozamine has been used to treat this condition as well.

Dietary management is the best way to prevent this condition in your Lorikeets. Better diets are available for Lorikeets these days. All you need to do is consult your vet. Bottled water is recommended if your bird has had this condition in the past.

Birds that have not had hemochromatosis and have lived long loves have been given a lot of fresh foods and low amounts of seeds. It is best that you also rely on a balanced diet for your birds to prevent the above mentioned nutritional deficiency.

If you are new to the world of Lorikeets it is recommended that you follow a diet provided by your vet to the T. As you gain more experience with your birds and do your own research, you can mix up the diet. In any case, remember that supplementation without consultation is always prohibited for your birds if you want to ensure that they stay in the best of their health for the rest of their lives.

b.Bacterial diseases

It is very common for birds to develop bacterial diseases. Most often inappropriate husbandry is responsible for making the birds develop these condition. Improper nutrition leads to compromised immunity that makes the birds more susceptible to these infections.

Juvenile birds and neonates are even more susceptible to these conditions. The respiratory tract and the gastrointestinal tract are the first ones to get affected by these bacteria.

There are various strains of bacteria that affect birds out of which strep, staph, citobacter and E.coli are the most common ones. These are the bacteria that are associated with humid areas, dust, old food, seed, grit and water. In some birds natural resistance to these bacteria may be compromised due to reproductive diseases in the parent.

Most common symptoms of bacterial infection

- Droppings that are watery and green in color.
- Sneezing
- Rubbing the eyes incessantly

- Swallowing constantly
- Coughing
- Yawning
- Coughing
- Change in voice or loss of voice

Bacterial infections, caused by either ingestion or inhalation is life threatening if left unattended. The exact type of bacteria needs to be identified before giving the bird any form of treatment. That it is when you can treat it perfectly and also prevent it from recurring.

Treatment and precautions for common bacterial diseases
- Antibiotics are administered after the culture test is complete.
- Antibiotic drops are given directly to the bird if he is very ill. You can even inject the antibiotics in these cases.
- If the infection is mild, you can administer the antibiotics through drinking water. You need to make sure that the bird is drinking water when you take this approach.

- All the seed, fruit and grit should be removed from the cage.

- Disinfecting the cage on a regular basis is a must.

- The seeds that you provide must be sterile.

- The bird must never be left out of the cage unsupervised.

- If your bird has not recovered fully, you need to make sure that you do not allow him to wander around the house.

There are several things that you can do in order to accelerate recovery in your bird. You can give the birds Turbo-boosters and also energy supplements.

Special Fvite with sterile seeds can be included as a part of the diet of your bird.

Once your antibiotic treatment is complete, you can give your bird loford and dufoplus in water. You need to make sure that your bird is eating and drinking well. If he is not doing so, your vet may have to force feed him.

Bacterial infections can become very severe in the long run. They will damage the kidney and liver if ignored and the bird becomes susceptible to a lot of illnesses in the future.

It is the responsibility of the owner to understand how a certain disease originated in order to help the bird recover faster. In order to ensure that your bird does not have repetitive episodes of infection you can get a complete health program from your vet and follow it till your bird is fully recovered.

Paying attention to bacterial infections is very important as humans can also be affected by certain strains of bacteria. The droppings of the bird can spread bacteria. Children are especially susceptible to infection and must be kept away from a sick bird. One example of a bacterial strain that affects Lorikeets and humans is campylobacter.

Remember that bacterial infections are usually related to the surroundings of the bird. If there is any contamination that enters the mouth of the bird, it will lead to the disorder.

Of course, even the best kept birds may be susceptible to infections. If this happens, it becomes even more important for you to make sure that you understand the source of the infection and try your best to prevent any more in the future.

Here are a few strains of bacteria and the common sources of infection for each one of them.

E.coli :
- Fluctuation of temperature
- Draught
- Stress
- Contaminated food or old fruit
- Wet areas
- Dirty cages

Strep
- Underlying viral infection
- Cold stress
- Dust
- Poor quality of food

- Stress

Staph
- Mice
- Dust
- Poor seed quality
- Contamination in the air conditioning

Diplococcus
- Stress
- Mice

Citobacter and Pseudomonas
- Poor water conditions
- Poor cage hygiene

Many owners believe in a holistic approach to prevent these infections. You may also try the following after consultation with your vet.

- **Goldensea:** This herb is used for its strong antibiotic property. It is effective against E.coli, staph and strep.

- **Echinacea :** This herb is known for killing several pathogens that cause diseases including protozoa, fungi and bacteria.

- **Licorice root:** This herb is antiviral and antibacterial in nature and is known to be effective against the most powerful strain of bacteria.

Most common bacterial conditions in Lorikeets

In case of Lorikeets, there are two conditions that you need to be extra cautious about. These birds are genetically predisposed to these conditions and may even be carriers of the condition in some cases.

Chlamydiosis

This is a condition that affects almost all companion birds. It is best that you follow all the federal regulations with respect to testing and quarantining for this condition if you plan to have an aviary or if you plan to breed Lorikeets.

This condition is caused by a type of bacteria called *chlamydia psittaci*. The incubation period of this strain ranges from 3 days to a couple of weeks.

The only concern with this condition is that it is easily transmitted from one bird to another through the feces. They bacteria stays infectious in debris that is organic for more than one month.

Symptoms in birds that are carriers:

- Anorexia
- Nasal and ocular discharge
- Dehydration
- Excessive droppings
- Lack of appetite
- Diarrhea

Symptoms in birds that are clinically ill:
- All of the above
- Monoystosis
- Leukocystosis
- Increase in bile acid level

Diagnosis
Diagnosis of this condition is quite difficult as the clinical signs are usually mild or absent. The most common methods of diagnosis include:
- Antigen and antibody tests
- Serological tests
- PCR testing
- Cloacal swab analysis

Multiple diagnosis methods must be applied because of the nature of this condition which is actually quite hard to identify and understand.

Treatments

- Doxycycline is the most common treatment option.
- Dietary calcium must be reduced during this treatment phase.
- Medicated feed may be administered if the condition is too severe.

You need to make sure that you devise a proper treatment plan for this condition as it can be transmitted to people quite easily.

Avian mycobacterosis
This condition is usually caused by different types of bacteria including *Mycobacterium avium, M.intercellulare, M.bovis, M.genovense and M.tuberculosis.*

This condition is progressive and usually affects the gastrointestinal tract of the bird as well as the liver. This condition is hard to diagnose because of the limited number of clinical signs available in the initial stages of infection.

Symptoms of Avian mycobacteriosis
- Weight loss
- Anorexia
- Diarrhea
- Depression

Diagnosis of the condition
- Acid fast staining of the culture
- Biopsy of the intestines, liver and spleen
- PCR testing
- Ultrasound

The difficult part in diagnosis is the fact that these strains of bacteria are very hard to culture. Therefore if the culture test is negative it is not conclusive that the condition does not exist.

The other tests are not as sensitive. The best option is PCR testing of a sample of the bird's feces. In some cases radiographs have been useful in determining the condition.

If you have an aviary with multiple birds, it is also hard to determine which of the birds is actually infected. If you are able to point out the birds that have the highest risk of being affected, you need to make sure that they are isolated and properly monitored.

Treatment
- Antibiotic treatment for 1 year or more
- Administration of multiple antibiotics
- Examination of your own husbandry practices

If your bird is in the advanced stage of this condition, it is less likely that he or she will be able survive. Although there have been no records of the conditions being passed on from birds to humans, you need to make sure that you take all the necessary precautions especially if you have an immunity that is weak.

c. Viral diseases

Viral infections in birds can be fatal in most conditions. Makings sure that your birds are checked by a vet on a regular basis is the key to keeping birds away from these diseases. With most viral diseases, the incubation period is very short and the birds may succumb to the infection overnight.

Here are some of the avian viral diseases that may affect Lorikeets:

Avian polyomavirus

This condition usually affects birds that are young. Usually adult birds are immune and in case of any infection, will shed the virus in just 90 days. Incubation period for avian polyomavirus is 10 days.

Symptoms of avian polyomavirus infection

In the most typical cases, a healthy juvenile bird that is still not a fledgling will develop crop stasis, lethargy and will die in just 48 hours of the onset of the condition. In rare cases, the following symptoms are recorded:

- Abdominal distention
- Cutaneous hemorrhage
- Feather abnormality

Diagnosis of the condition
- Examination of the cloacal swab
- Blood tests
- Virus neutralizing tests
- Antibody tests
- Necropsy testing of the chicks that have succumbed to the condition.

Prevention of the condition
- Keeping the aviary free from visitors.
- Making sure that new birds are only included in the aviary after 90 days of strict quarantining.
- Making sure that you keep up all the practices of hygiene.

- Stopping breeding for at least six months if the condition is diagnosed in any bird in the aviary.
- Disinfection of the nesting boxes and the aviary.
- Avoid purchasing birds from different sources.
- Avoid purchasing birds that have still not been weaned.

Treatment of the condition

As discussed before avian polyomavirus has a very short incubation period and the symptoms are rarely seen before the bird succumbs to the infection.

You can opt for a vaccine that is available for younger birds. Making sure that you give birds that are breeding a dose of these vaccine at intervals of two weeks in the off season in a must.

You must also provide these vaccines to neonates before they are 35 days old. You have the option of a booster shot after about 3 weeks as well. Getting your birds this shot prevents the risk of infection to a large extent.

In general, there is no cure for this condition except preventive measures and supportive care after the condition has been diagnosed.

Gouldian Finch Herpesvirus
This is a rather uncharacterized strain of virus that is known to affect Lorikeets, Crimson Lorikeets and Red faced waxbills. If you have an aviary with multiple birds, you will observe lesions in birds that are affected. However, some of them may be completely unaffected by the virus.

Symptoms of Finch Herpesvirus
- Listlessness
- Ruffled plumes
- Heavy breathing
- Nasal discharge
- Swelling in the eyelids
- Crusts in the cleft of the eyelid
- Inability to eat

After about 5-10 days of the first signs and symptoms of this viral infection, it has been observed that birds are unable to survive. Post necropsy, it was observed that the birds showed thickening of the fibnoid and discharge in the eyes and nostrils. Besides that the internal organs seemed normal on all occasions.

Herpes virus are considered an alpha strain of virus because of which the incubation period is very short and the damage caused is quite serious. There is no cure for these conditions. All you can do is take preventive measures to make sure that the birds are quarantined properly, given ample food and clean water and are kept in the most hygienic conditions possible.

Avian bornavirus

Infections by avian bornavirus in birds were observed quite recently in birds with the first ever records being made in the 1970s. Since then, several species have been considered susceptible to the condition including Lorikeets. The first evidence of this condition affecting Lorikeets was observed in Estrildid Lorikeets.

This condition is progressive in a few cases or may develop overnight in others. Mortality rates are high in birds that have been affected by this strain of virus.

After several crop biopsies, it was discovered that affected birds have lesions in the heart, the gastrointestinal tract, the brain, spinal cord, lungs and kidneys. The disease may either be transmitted orally or through the feces. It is highly contagious and can be even more problematic if you have a mixed aviary.

Symptoms of avian bornavirus infections:
- Chronic weight loss
- Increase in appetite followed by excretion of undigested food
- Regurgitation
- Convulsions
- Weakness
- Tremors
- Ataxia or inability to control movements
- Blindness

Diagnosis
- Biopsy of cloacal swabs
- PCR testing

These tests need to be carried out once every week for three straight weeks to determine if the bird is really infected or not. The virus is shed intermittently which makes it even more necessary for you to have multiple tests as well as differential diagnosis for conditions like toxicosis and foreign body obstruction before the conclusions are derived for infection by the avian bornavirus.

Treatment
- Providing the bird with food that is easy to digest
- Administering medications likecelecoxib and meloxicam
- Isolation of infected birds as a method of disease prevention
- Regular PCR tests
- Good hygiene
- Ultraviolet light setting

Poxvirus infection
This is a large DNA virus that usually affects the respiratory tract, the oral cavity and the epithelial cells of the internal organs. It is believed that all birds are susceptible to this condition. In case of aviary birds or companion birds, this condition can be avoided as the birds will not be exposed to this virus if proper husbandry practices are followed.

This disease usually affects parrots and Lorikeets. In case of Lorikeets, your bird may only be a carrier and may never develop symptoms. However, for those with a mixed aviary, this is also cause for great concern as the disease spreads rapidly.

The infection may be cutaneous or systemic depending upon the strain of virus that has affected your bird, the age of your bird, the health of the bird and the route of exposure.

In the cutaneous form, you will notice that there are wart like growths on parts of the body that are unfeathered including the area around the eyes and nares, the legs and the beak. Another form which is the diptheric form shows similar formations on the larynx, pharynx, tongue and the mucosa. The systemic form is differentiated by the characteristic ruffled appearance of the bird.

Symptoms of poxvirus infection
- Lesions on the eye, ear and oral cavity
- Lethargy

- Troubled or labored breathing
- Difficulty in swallowing
- Partial blindness
- Weight loss
- Skin lesions
- Ruffled appearance

Treatment of poxvirus infection
- Supportive care
- Fluids included in the diet
- Vitamin A supplementation
- Cleaning of the lesions on a daily basis
- Antibiotics
- Ointments for secondary infections
- Assisted feeding
- Mosquito control
- Indoor housing

It is also possible to provide your Lorikeets with certain vaccinations that will make them immune to certain strains of pox virus.

Avian influenza
Commonly known as bird flu, this is a condition that affects almost all species of birds. Most of the causal strains of virus do not affect human beings. However, it was recently discovered that some strains like the A(H7N9) cause serious infections in humans as well.

This is a condition that commonly affects waterfowl but can even lead to outbreaks on a large scale in an aviary set up. The virus is so potent that it has the ability to even affect other mammals. So if you have other pets at home, you have to be very careful and watchful.

This diseases has a very aggressive progression. This means that the disease can spread within a few hours and can lead to death as well.

Symptoms of avian influenza
- High fever
- Diarrhea
- Vomiting
- Coughing

- Abdominal distension
- Decreased egg production
- Inflammation of the trachea
- Congestion
- Hemorrhage
- Edema
- Lack of limb coordination
- Paralysis
- Blood in the nasal and oral discharge
- Greenish color of the droppings

Treatment
- Vaccination is the best option to prevent the disease altogether

This condition can be serious if the strain of virus that affects the bird can affect humans as well. In many states it is a mandate to report the outbreak of avian influenza in your aviary to a regulatory authority. Your avian vet should be able to help you with this.

In most cases, antiviral compounds cannot be administered to the bird unless it is approved by these regulatory authorities. Even the vaccination that is used on your birds needs to be approved by the USDA or by the state veterinarian.

d.Diseases caused by parasites
There are both endo and ectoparasites that can affect Lorikeets. These parasites are mostly found in unhygienic conditions. While they are not always fatal, there are chances that the symptoms only become obvious when the bird is already very unwell. That is the only reason why parasitic infections are a threat to the bird's life. In most cases, a bird seems completely normal and the symptoms become severe overnight.

Here are a few parasitic infections that Lorikeets are most susceptible to:

Coccidiosis

This condition is caused by a certain parasite that is usually found in the intestinal tract of birds. The disease is transmissible and is passed on through the feces or through interaction. The condition is highly contagious and you will notice several birds being infected immediately after you notice the first case in your aviary.

Symptoms of coccidiosis

- The vent area is wet
- The bird has consistent diarrhea
- The feathers are fluffed up
- The bird has very little energy when you approach him
- The bird tends to sleep a lot

Treatment

- A course of sulfonamide or sulphadim is required
- The cage needs to be cleaned regularly to prevent any sort of infestation in your aviary.
- The drinking containers should be made only from glass or plastic while providing any antibiotics
- You may continue a course of broad spectrum antibiotics.

Parasitic worms

If your bird is being fed any live foods, worms are easily picked up. It is therefore necessary for you to make sure that the live food that you give your bird is fresh.

Another source of parasitic worms is the droppings of birds in the aviary. If the parent bird is a carrier of parasites, they may transfer it to the young while feeding.

When you have an outdoor cage, you need to make sure that there are no droppings of wild birds in your aviary. This is the primary source of several parasites and infectious diseases.

Symptoms of parasitical worms

- Weakness
- Worms are spotted in the feces of birds
- Worms are seen in the water dishes

The disease is fatal only when the condition is not treated properly. The most common worms that affect Lorikeets are threadworms, caecal worms, tapeworms, gapeworms, tapeworms and roundworms.

Treatment:

- Have a routine worm management program for your bird
- A broad spectrum wormer like levamisole can be administered to the bird

- Have your birds tested regularly

Scaly face
This is a condition that is also known as Knemidocoptes jamaiscensis. When mites borrow into the feathers of the bird and lay eggs there, this condition is caused.

The condition gets worse when the eggs that have been laid in the feathers actually hatch. The most common way of transmission for this condition is when the parent birds feed the young. It has been observed in adult birds as well but the source of transmission is not very well known.

Symptoms of scaly face
- A scaly film is seen on the skin
- The scales may be formed on the eyes if left untreated
- Scales are seen on the legs of the bird

If you ignore this condition it will become fatal as the scales will slowly spread all over the body. The parasites are demanding and will lead to the death of the host.

Treatment
- Paraffin is administered to birds that have been affected by this condition.

Air sac mites
This is one of the most common conditions that you will see in Lorikeets. The mite that causes this condition is scientifically called *Sternostoma tracheacolum.*

The condition affects the respiratory system of your bird, leading to a lot of labored breathing. The disease is transmitted during courtship and also when the parents feed their young.

Symptoms of air sac mites
- Coughing
- Loss of voice
- Abnormal chirping
- Labored breathing
- Fatigue

Treatment
- An insecticide is used to eradicate the mites fully.
- A spray containing ivermectin can be used in the cage.
- All birds, including the ones that are not affected should be treated for air sac mites.

These parasites have a life cycle of 6 days before which you need to make sure that your bird is treated. If the eggs hatch before treatment, the process becomes a lot more tedious and the condition progresses rapidly.

e.Accidents and injuries
Birds are always prone to accidents and injuries, especially when they are in an aviary. If you let your birds outside the cage, there are several things that can lead to accidents such as sharp edges of furniture, closed windows or even doors.

If your bird does suffer from an injury when he is moving around the house of if he has a fight with another bird, providing timely first aid is the key to helping your bird recover faster.

Broken wings

Broken wings are a very common injury with birds because of the fragile nature of their bones. With Lorikeets, flight is the only mode of exercise and defense. When the wings of these birds are broken and not set properly, they tend to compromise the flight of the bird forever.

It is best that you take professional assistance if you have no experience with birds. However, providing first aid can relieve a lot of pain. If the wound is accompanied by open cuts or bruises, it is best that you call your vet immediately.

Helping a bird with broken wings

If your bird is stumbling on the floor of the cage and is holding one wing lower than the other, it could be signs of a broken wing. Here are a few things you can do if you suspect that your bird has a broken wing.

- Pick up your bird and put him carrier. The bird must be shifted to an area that is quiet and secluded.

- Once the bird has calmed down, check his body for any other injuries. In case of any cuts, you can clean it with an antibacterial solution.

- In case of profuse bleeding, dabbing some cornstarch on the wound can really help the bird.

- Cut a 12 inch strip of bandaging tape. This is the best option as it will not stick to the feather of the bird.

- Pick the bird up and gently hold the wing that is broken against the body of the bird.
- The bandage should be tight enough to hold the wing in place and can be secured under the wing that is intact.

- Let the bird walk around after the wing has been taped. If he is unable to walk or if he is unable to breathe, you may have to adjust the bandage.

- The bandage should be left on for about 4 weeks. You can consult your vet in order to provide the bird with supplements to aid the healing process.

- If the bird is unable to fly even after 4 week, he will have to be rehabilitated at a local facility.

Cuts and bruises

There are several causes for bruises and cuts in case of birds. Usually when a blood feather breaks, it bleeds quite profusely. This is the easiest form of bruise to heal.

Helping a bird with a broken blood feather

- The first thing you need to do is control the bleeding. Styptic powder or flour can help control bleeding.

- If that does not help, hold the wound down with gauze and apply a little pressure. This will keep the bleeding down till you take the bird to a good vet.

- The bleeding shaft is usually pulled out to prevent blood loss. You may do this at home if you have experience with birds. If not, it is best that you take your finch to the vet.

The next most common cause for injury is attacks by cats or dogs. This causes a lot of stress to the bird and you need to be extra cautious when dealing with this sort of injury.

Helping a bird who has been attacked

- Take him to a quiet room and keep him warm. This will help him recover from the shock of being attacked.

- In case the wound is bleeding, you can control it by applying pressure with a piece of gauze. But, be sure that you are not hampering breathing in any way.

- The bird must be taken to the vet immediately in order to avoid any chances of infection. Cat saliva is very toxic for birds.

- You need to check for any broken bones. In case of broken or wings, you can wrap them at home and then take the bird to the vet. In case of broken skull or legs, you must never try to clean it up at home.

Burns

A bird can suffer from burns accidentally if they land on a hot stove or if they touch a hot table lamp while flying around the house. It is very important that owners make it a priority to make their home safe for the bird to live in.

However, in case your bird does suffer from burns despite all the precautions, your bird will require first aid.

Helping a bird with scalds

Scalds are caused by hot liquids, chemicals and fire. In case this accident occurs in your home:

- First wash the burn with cold water and flush it for about 115 minutes.

- If it is a third degree burn, you have to rush your bird to the vet. On the way to the vey, you need to cover the affected area with moistened gauze pads.

- Contact lens saline is one of the most effective ways to cool down a burn as long as it is preservative free.

Helping a bird with electric burns

This is very rare in Lorikeets as they do not have beaks that are strong enough to bite through electric wires. Nevertheless, they may come in contact with exposed live wires that may lead to the burn. Here is what you can do if your bird has an unfortunate accident:

- Do not touch the bird till you get the bird out of contact with the electrical wire. This puts you also at the risk of electrocution. Turn the electrical source off before you do anything.

- Check the breathing of your birds as well as the heartbeat. It is advisable that you learn basic CPR techniques for birds from your vet.

- Call the emergency clinic immediately. When you are taking your bird to the facility, make sure that you keep him in a container that is warm and dark. You can use a plastic bag filled with warm water to give the bird the warmth it requires.

What you must NEVER do in case of burs
- Never apply ice on the burnt area
- Butter, ointment and grease should never be applied.
- If there are any wounds with debris, do not attempt to clean them.
- Blisters should not be popped.
- Never cover a burn with a towel or any material that has fibres which may stick to the wound.
- If the bird is unconscious, do not give him any oral medications or even water.

After the bird has been treated makes sure that you give him all he IV fluids and electrolytes mentioned by the vet on a regular basis. Antibiotics should be provided as required to make sure that your bird heals fast

Toxicosis

Toxicosis or heavy metal poisoning is very common in birds. This is mostly because birds are easily poisoned by certain heavy metals like lead, zinc and iron that are found in their environment.

Each of the metals affects the birds in a different way but every one of them is equally hazardous to the bird and must be treated immediately.

Today, people are more aware of the potential issues related to metal poisoning. They take a lot more precautions to make sure that their birds are not at the risk of developing any form of toxicosis.

Like humans, birds also contain a moderate amount of zinc and iron in their body. These minerals are present in their food and are actually necessary for metabolism to occur normally. However, when the levels of these minerals increase to an abnormal level, toxicosis occurs.

Lead poisoning is the least common type of heavy metal poisoning today as most of the pet owners take precautions. You also have better quality toys and enclosures that prevent toxicity in birds.

In case the level of iron increases in the body of your bird, it leads to iron storage disease. This leads to excessive iron deposits on the internal organs of the bird. This leads to problems in the liver and can potentially damage the other organs permanently.

Symptoms of toxicosis

- Tremors
- Constant thirst
- Regurgitation of consumed water
- Listlessness
- Fatigue
- Depression
- Lack of coordination in the muscles
- Seizures

Diagnosis of toxicosis
- An X-ray of the gizzard helps identify the type of metal that has affected the bird.
- Blood tests are necessary to detect heavy metal poisoning
- If you suspect any chances of heavy metal poisoning, it is necessary that you take your bird to the vet immediately.

Treatment
- There are certain organic compounds called chelates that are used to detoxify any poisoning in the bird.
- These agents can be injected directly into the muscles of the bird to make sure that the blood level returns to normal.

- After the bird recovers from the condition, you can provide oral chelating agents.

The speed of recovery depends entirely on the level of poisoning. You can take preventive measures as well:

- Make sure that you remove any material such as the fencing or the perches and cages that may contain lead or iron.

- Stainless steel is the best option to prevent toxicosis in birds.

- When your bird is playing outside the cage, you need to ensure that no heavy metal is available for the bird to consume.

- Keep stained glass, old paints, fishing weights and lead curtains away from the bird's environment.

- You must also make sure that your bird does not come in contact with any soldered parts or areas.

f.Reproductive diseases

There are a few complications that may occur when your birds reach the breeding age. Particularly in the hens, there are several problems related to the formation of the eggs and the laying of eggs that you need to be aware of in order to have a healthy clutch.

Egg yolk peritonitis

This condition leads to the presence of some egg yolk in the coelomic cavity. The egg yolk is one of the best mediums for bacteria to thrive in and is usually caused by a prior bacterial infection.

The response is inflammatory and you will be able to see abdominal distension in birds that deal with this condition. In most cases, diagnosis is only possible after the death of the bird.

There are several other conditions that occur with egg yolk peritonitis including oviduct prolapse, double yolks, internal laying of the egg and internal ovulation.

You need to make sure that you follow the right lighting recommendations for your bird and also provide them with the nutrition that they require in order to lay the eggs successfully.

This condition is very common in birds that are overweight or have erratic periods of ovulation.

Symptoms of egg yolk peritonitis

- Loss of appetite
- Respiratory distress
- Fluffing of feathers
- Loss of voice or vocalization
- Depression
- Weakness
- Swollen vent
- Swollen abdomen
- Ascites

When the bird shows the symptoms, it is usually accompanied by very obvious nesting symptoms. Diagnosis upon the death of the bird reveals that the fluids contain ascites which are not present in healthy specimens of Lorikeets.

This condition usually ends in the death of the bird and is sudden or very quick in progression.

Chronic egg laying

Birds require certain nesting conditions in order to breed and lay eggs. The factors that contribute the most towards stimulating a bird to lay eggs are:
- Rainfall
- Behavior of the mate
- Availability of food
- Length of the day
- Competition for nesting areas

If the ideal conditions are available, female Lorikeets do not even have to mate with a partner in order to lay the eggs. This leads to a condition known as chronic egg laying which can lead to other complications such as calcium depletion or hypocalcemia as well as egg binding.

Preventing chronic egg laying

You can make sure that your bird does not lay eggs by making the ideal conditions unavailable. Here are a few things that you can do:

- Allow your bird to sit on the eggs and hatch them. If you take away the eggs as soon as they are laid, she may continue to lay them. It is advised to leave the eggs in the cage until the bird loses interest in them.

- Nesting material should be removed from the cage. Things like paper and small dark places like boxes or sleeping tents should be removed. If your bird is let out of the cage, discourage him from going behind the microwave, under the table etc. where it is dark and cozy. They may even turn this into a nesting area if you do not pay enough attention.

- Keep the lights in the living area of the birds dim. It is good to increase the dark hours to make the bird feel like the days have become shorter. This will turn their breeding hormones off and will make them sleep for longer.

- Food access can be limited. In the wild, birds will never breed unless they have ample food. If your bird has the habit of laying eggs too often, you can reduce the amount of time that food is available. Instead of keeping the food bowl filled all day, you can reduce the time of food availability to 12 hours. If that does not work, you can speak to your vet to give your bird an austerity diet which is very low in protein. Giving your bird this diet for about 2 weeks will discourage breeding and egg laying.

- Do not encourage any breeding behavior in your birds. Lifting the tail, rubbing the vent etc. should be avoided. Make sure your birds get good exercise and keep them engaged.
- If nothing works, you can give your bird a hormonal injection after consulting your vet.

The one thing that you need to remember when your bird displays excessive egg laying is that it causes a rapid depletion in the nutrients in the body. Consulting your vet to provide your bird with necessary supplements can help prevent secondary health conditions and infections.

Egg binding

This is a very common but potentially hazardous conditions for birds. When the female bird is not able to pass the egg through the cloaca, this condition occurs. Sometimes, the egg may be painfully lodged deeper into the reproductive tract. This condition is most common in small sized birds such as Lorikeets. If the egg breaks internally, it may even lead to the death of the bird.

There are several causal factors for egg binding such as:
- Low levels of calcium in the blood
- Limited sunlight
- Unavailability of vitamin D3 in the diet
- Malnutrition
- Lack of exercise
- Small cages that do not permit movement
- Age of the bird
- Prior illness
- Solitary laying of the eggs

Symptoms of egg binding
- Depression
- Straining of the abdomen
- Fluffed feathers
- Loss of appetite
- Abnormal droppings
- Inability to excrete

A bird with egg binding must be taken to a vet immediately. If your vet is able to feel the egg through a regular physical examination, then it is removed easily. In case the egg is deeper in the reproductive tract, an X ay is necessary to determine the condition.

Treatment
- If you have any doubt that the bird may have egg binding, you could keep her in a warm room. A steam room or even a warm towel can help relax the vent of the bird and aid the passing of the egg.
- A shallow water bath with warm water will help the bird to a large extent.
- Provide the bird with calcium supplementation.
- You may apply a lubricant in order to aid the passing of the egg. Coconut oil can be of great assistance.

This is a condition that can be potentially life threatening. Taking preventive measures is the best way to help your Lorikeet. You can provide your bird with a regular dose of calcium shots. In case you want to safeguard your bird from this condition, having them spayed is an option. If that is not an option, you can also ensure that the right breeding requirements are not available to the bird.

Your vet should also be able to provide your bird with Lupron shots which will prevent the breeding hormones from being produced.

3. Preventive measures

There is no better way to keep your bird healthy than preventive care. Since most illnesses spread so fast in Lorikeet birds, it is best that you take all the precautionary steps possible to prevent this sort of infection in the first place. Here are some tips that will help you maintain the health of your little feathered companion:

- Make sure that the diet is wholesome and nutritious

- Clean the cage and its contents regularly

- Take your pet to the vet for an annual checkup without fail

- Any new bird that is introduced to your home must be quarantined without fail

- The bird must have a lot of clean water to drink

- Your Lorikeet must be mentally stimulated in order to ensure good health

- Spend enough time with your bird to prevent any behavioral problems

- You need to make sure that he gets ample sunlight. It is a good idea to take the bird outdoors provided he is harnessed or is protected by a cage.

- Your home must be bird proofed even before you bring the bird home.

- Grooming and cleaning the bird is necessary.

Always keep your vet's number handy and learn as much as you can about your Lorikeet's health. That way, communicating with the vet also becomes easier and you will be able to provide better care for your bird.

Chapter 8) Cost of Owning a Lorikeet

Let us take a look at the monetary responsibility that you will be taking on by bringing a Lorikeet home.

- Cost of the Lorikeet: $100-800 or £50 to 500 depending upon the age, type, the breeding conditions and the source that you but them from.
- Cage: $150- 400 or £80- 200 depending upon the features available and the size. This is a one- time investment and it is recommended that you get the best.
- Food: $40 or £25 every month.
- Toys: This really depends upon the type of toys that you buy. But you will shell out a minimum of $15 or £10 on each toy that you buy.
- Veterinarian Cost: You will spend at least $50 or £30 per visit to your veterinarian. You can expect annual costs of about $1200 or £650 per year.
- Pet Insurance: Depending on the kinds of covers that you are getting, your pet insurance may cost anything between $150- 280 or £80- 150 every month.

In all, you need to keep aside a minimum of $450- 500 or £200-250 every month to provide proper care for your bird. You must never make any compromises in this respect and ensure that your bird gets the best life.

If you have any doubts about being able to support your bird, wait for a time when you know that you can give him or her better care. That will make the whole experience with your Lorikeet more fulfilling instead of causing unwanted stress and irritation.

Think ahead and make your budget plans for at least five years before you bring a Lorikeet home. In case you see anything in the future like a marriage or a baby that can increase your financial responsibilities, see if your Lorikeet would fit into it too. The expense is one of the biggest factors that causes owners to give up their Lorikeets. This can be very traumatic for the bird and, indeed, very bitter for the owner.

So, it is best that you make a good budget that may even include a few savings for your Lorikeet every month to help you deal with any emergency.

Conclusion

Lorikeets can be quite a handful if you are a first time bird owner. However, they are also extremely delightful pets to have. Thank you for choosing this book as a first step into the world of Lorikeets.

The more you interact with your bird, the more you will learn about his quirky ways, his peculiar habits and also his specific needs. You can adapt based on what you learn from your own bird to make sure that you provide the best possible care to your bird.

The idea behind this book is to give you a head start so that you know exactly what to expect. Make sure that you read up about Lorikeets, learn about them from other Lorikeet owners and also try to stay updated about health care with information from your veterinarian's office.

With this book, you will certainly gain a good insight into being a good Lorikeet parent. Here is wishing you a wonderful journey with your bird who will love you and, without a doubt, add a whole new dimension to your   life.

References

As mentioned before, there is no end to how much you can learn about your bird. There is a host of blogs, forums and websites online that you can check regularly for more information on Lorikeet care. Here are some references that you can use when you need any tips about Lorikeet care, behavior or health.

Note: at the time of printing, all the websites below were working. As the internet changes rapidly, some sites might no longer be live when you read this book. That is, of course, out of our control.

www.forums.avianavenue.com

www.vcahospitals.com

www.cuteness.com

www.parrotsociety.org.au

www.birdtricksstore.com

www.birdwatchingblog.us

www.goodbirdinc.blogspot.com

www.nashvillezoo.org/our-blog

www.blogs.thatpetplace.com

www.roadlesstravelled.com.au

www.aquariumofpacific.org

www.windycityparrot.com

www.okczoo.org

www.birdchannel.com

www.webvet.com

http://www.featherme.com/

http://www.merckvetmanual.com/

http://www.peteducation.com/

http://www.webvet.com/

http://www.parrotscanada.com/

www.pets4homes.co.uk

www.beautyofbirds.com

www.birds.about.com

www.birdchannel.com

www.petsuppliesplus.com

www.animal-world.com

www.goodbirdinc.com

www.associationofanimalbehaviorprofessionals.com

www.pets.thenest.com

www.ingramcontent.com/pod-product-compliance
Lightning Source LLC
Chambersburg PA
CBHW060121050426
42448CB00010B/1985